"One of the first books I tell new writers to buy. It is indispensable, practical, readable, and fun to use. Buy this book before you write another word! "
— Dean Batali, TV Writer/Producer (*That '70s Show*, *Buffy the Vampire Slayer*)

"Required reading for any screenwriter who wants to be taken seriously by Hollywood. Can't imagine how there never has been a book like this before! "
— Elizabeth Stephen, President, Television; Executive Vice President, Motion Picture Production, Mandalay Television Pictures

"It doesn't matter how great your screenplay is if it looks all wrong. *The Hollywood Standard* is probably the most critical book any screenwriter who is serious about being taken seriously can own. For any writer who truly understands the power of making a good first impression, this comprehensive guide to format and style is priceless."
— Marie Jones, Book Reviewer, www.absolutewrite.com

"Christopher Riley just made my job tougher! Each year experienced producers screen out hundreds of scripts because the mistakes in form and organization reveal them to be the work of amateurs. But if those hopeful writers follow Riley's concise and knowledgeable advice, they're going to look like the best professionals in Hollywood."
— Robert W. Cort, Producer (*Save the Last Dance*, *Runaway Bride*, *Mr. Holland's Opus*, *The Hand That Rocks the Cradle*, *Three Men and a Baby*, *Outrageous Fortune*)

"In Hollywood, looks matter. Read *The Hollywood Standard* to ensure that your script not only gets in past the Hollywood bouncers, but turns heads when it gets there."
— Amy Snow, winner, 2004 ABC/Disney Screenwriting Fellowship

"Riley has succeeded in an extremely difficult task: he has produced a guide to screenplay formatting which is both entertaining to read and exceptionally thorough. Riley's clear style, authoritative voice and well-written examples make this book far more enjoyable than any formatting guide has a right to be. This is the best guide to script formatting ever, and it is an indispensable tool for every writer working in Hollywood."
— Wout Thielemans, *Screentalk*

THE HOLLYWOOD STANDARD

THE COMPLETE AND AUTHORITATIVE GUIDE TO SCRIPT FORMAT AND STYLE

BY CHRISTOPHER RILEY

CONTENTS

INTRODUCTION

Welcome to the most accurate, complete, authoritative, and practical guide to standard script formats ever published, written by a guy who came to Hollywood to make his career as a screenwriter and instead accidentally became Hollywood's foremost authority on industry standard script formats.

How does a thing like that happen?

Shortly after I arrived in Los Angeles, I took a job proofreading scripts in Warner Bros' acclaimed script processing department, in those days literally a 24-hour-a-day script factory. For fourteen years I worked alongside veterans the studio had lured away from Barbara's Place, the legendary Hollywood script house, learning and applying standard format rules to untold thousands of scripts. I ultimately ran the department as the historic studio's premier format guru. I wrote the script typing software the studio used to type countless scripts and served as the ultimate arbiter of format for that studio and for dozens of outside clients that included Amblin, Disney, Columbia, Universal, NBC Productions, Wilshire Court Productions, and many more. And, arguably, I ended up knowing more about script format than anyone in Hollywood.

I've since found my way into a screenwriting career. I've walked the red carpet at the premier of my first film in Berlin. I've written movies for Touchstone and Paramount, Mandalay and Intermedia. I've also become a successful screenwriting instructor. And I've seen how badly we screenwriters need a reliable, easy-to-use format guide.

THE MISSING BOOK

Until now, a genuinely accurate, complete, and practical guide to standard script formats has been impossible to find. Many books deal briefly with the subject. A few treat it at some length. But even the best-selling and best-intentioned of the earlier books are either outdated, inaccurate at many points, difficult to use, or incomplete. To fill the void, I offer this guide based on my experience at Warner Bros., intended to be kept at a screenwriter's fingertips and filled with clear, concise, complete formatting instructions, and hundreds of examples to take the guesswork out of a multitude of formatting questions that perplex screenwriters, waste their time, and steal their confidence.

"BUT I DON'T NEED A BOOK, I USE FINAL DRAFT"

Or Movie Magic Screenwriter. Or Scriptware. Or one of the other incredibly useful and time-saving script typing programs on the market. What else does a writer need?

To begin with, standard format is about infinitely more than margins. It's knowing when to add a shot heading and when to leave one out. It's knowing how to get out of a POV shot and how to set up a montage. It's knowing what to capitalize and how to control pacing and what belongs in parenthetical character direction and whether those automatic (cont'd)s beside dialogue should be turned on or off. No script typing software is designed to answer those questions. Consequently, too many writers who think they're turning in professionally formatted scripts are in fact often turning in scripts that brand them as amateurs.

THE FAN TEST

Stacks and stacks of scripts by first-timers and even professionals never receive serious consideration because they fail the fan test. Overworked readers, studio executives, agents, and producers pick up a script, flip to the last page and fan toward the front, looking at nothing but the physical layout of the script on the page. The format. What they see forms their first impression of your dream script. And sometimes their last. This guide tells you what you need to know to get your script past the fan test.

BUT THAT'S NOT ALL

The fan test isn't the only reason serious screenwriters need to master standard Hollywood format. Mark Twain was only joking when he said, "Anyone who can only think of one way to spell a word obviously lacks imagination." For the same reasons we need dictionaries and standardized spellings, we need standard formats. Not because we can't think of more than one way to lay out our vision on the page, but because we can think of too many.

The fact is that a standard format exists today in Hollywood and if we don't master it, if we rely only on our imaginations, we're bound to embarrass ourselves. Or appear ignorant. Or amateurish. Or confuse our readers because we haven't been clear. Or waste our time reinventing what already exists. A standard gives writers confidence that they're steering clear of all these dangers and frees them to think about more interesting things. Like their characters and stories.

WHERE STANDARD FORMAT CAME FROM

Pioneering filmmakers in Hollywood standardized screenplay format beginning as early as the 1920s. Look at a script from the silent era and you'll recognize the basic layout of the modern script page. With the addition of sound and dialogue, the format evolved. It evolved further when television arrived. But the truth is, the look of a script page in Hollywood has changed very little since the beginning.

During the 1960s and '70s, well before the appearance of the first PC and script writing software, screenplays and teleplays were being typed by large "mimeo" departments at studios and specialized script houses sprinkled around Hollywood. Probably the most important of these was Barbara's Place, a legendary script operation that turned out thousands of scripts over the years and whose typists and proofreaders became the industry's foremost guardians of standard script format.

By the early 1980s, that mantle passed to Warner Bros.' acclaimed script processing department where numerous Barbara's Place stalwarts migrated with their exhaustive knowledge of the Hollywood script business. The studio provided what was then state-of-the-art computer technology, and soon laser printers the size of Winnebagos were churning out scripts around the clock at the astonishing rate of 3 pages per second for television series like *The Dukes of Hazzard*, *Designing Women*, *Murphy Brown*, and *ER*, and movies like *Lethal Weapon*, *Batman*, *Forrest Gump*, *Rain Man*, *Unforgiven*, *Three Kings*, and *Twister*.

I joined the Warner Bros. staff as a neophyte script proofreader in 1983. I remained for fourteen years. During my years at Warner Bros., I was privileged to learn from Barbara's Place veterans Les Miller, Tim Alfors, Vern Hedges, Val Evensen, Kathleen Hietala, and Gordon Barclay, a group unrivaled in their mastery of script formats. Together with a staff of skilled typists and supervisors assembled by the studio, we applied what we knew to countless thousands of scripts, not just for Warner Bros., but for literally every studio in Hollywood.

The knowledge I gained during my years at Warner Bros. serves me every day. That is the knowledge I've set out to record in this guide and which I dare to call complete and authoritative, not as a boast but as a tribute to the unassailable credentials of those who taught me.

IS "THE HOLLYWOOD STANDARD" THE ONLY WAY?

Of course not. Good writers with long Hollywood careers will find details here with which to quibble. That's fine. The intent of this manual isn't to pick fights, condemn alternative approaches, or impose restrictions on anyone. The intent is simply to offer writers a set of time-honored guidelines that will help them produce scripts in a form that is highly-readable, clear, and professional.

USING THIS GUIDE

The Hollywood Standard is designed as a manual that every screenwriter, from neophyte to old pro, will want to keep within arm's reach. It's intended to be used as a reference, with the information organized for easy and immediate accessibility via the table of contents at the front of the book or the index at the back. You can spend just a short time reading through its pages and learn the basics, probably in something like an hour. Then, when you're in the throes of writing and need to see exactly how to set up a telescopic POV shot or review some fine point of handling camera direction, you can find the relevant guidelines and examples in a matter of seconds.

This guide doesn't cover story structure, character development, or dialogue. What it does cover is format and style, those components of a script that appear exclusively on the page and not the screen. Format is standard; style is personal and infinitely variable.

Throughout this guide, you'll find the rules of standard screenplay format. But you'll also find many examples of how to work within those rules to create your own crisp, professional, entertaining script-writing style. I hope you'll find it indispensable.

SINGLE-CAMERA FILM FORMAT

This is the classic screenplay format developed over decades of Hollywood history. It is used for productions filmed principally with one camera:

- theatrical feature films
- hour-long television drama
- long-form television, including made-for-television movies and miniseries

■ The four building blocks of single-camera film format

Despite their potential to map out film and television of soaring imagination, beauty and complexity, screenplays and teleplays consist of only four basic format elements: **shot headings**, **direction**, **dialogue**, and **transitions**.

Shot headings begin each new scene or shot. They may give general information about a scene's location and the time of day the scene takes place:

```
INT. PENTAGON - FIFTH FLOOR CORRIDOR - DAY
```

Or they may give information about the type and subject of a specific shot:

```
EXTREME CLOSEUP - WANDA'S TRIGGER FINGER
```

Shot headings are most often followed by *direction*, passages that describe what is being seen and heard within the shot or scene:

```
Micah crawls under the fence, the barbed wire
snagging his tattered jumpsuit.  The beam of a
searchlight passes and he presses himself into the
ground, desperate to make himself invisible.
```

Dialogue consists of the name of the character who is speaking, the actual words that are spoken, and any parenthetical character direction related to the dialogue:

```
                    MIMI
          That just figures, don't it?
               (smacks steering
                wheel)
          I go and steal me a car without
          no gas.
```

Transitions sometimes appear at the end of scenes and indicate how one scene links to the next:

```
                                        DISSOLVE TO:
```

See *Appendix A* for sample script pages in single-camera film format.

■ Margins and fonts for single-camera film format

Standard format dictates that scripts always use a *fixed-pitch font*, such as Courier or Courier New, and adhere to *standard margins*. A fixed-pitch font (as opposed to a proportionally spaced font like the one used in this paragraph) is one in which every letter occupies the same amount of horizontal space on the line, regardless of whether it is a lower case i or a capital M. Fonts used for typing scripts are 10 pitch, meaning there are 10 characters per horizontal inch, and 12 points, which allows six lines of type per vertical inch. Twelve-point Courier or Courier New fit the bill and are the fonts most often used in scripts. Used in combination with a fixed-pitch font, standard margins result in script pages with a relatively uniform amount of content per page.

Why is this important?

Over the years, a rule of thumb developed among filmmakers that one script page translated, on average, into one minute of finished film. Production cost estimates also came to be based in part on the number of pages in a script or scene. So did the amount of time allotted for filming scenes. Television writers knew that if they wrote roughly sixty pages, they had the right amount of material for a one-hour show. Feature writers knew that a 120-page screenplay represented a film of about two hours. And despite any number of quibbles one may have with these formulas (scripts for the brooding one-hour series *China Beach* often ran as few as fifty pages while scripts for the hyperkinetic *ER*, also an hour long, sometimes stretched up to seventy pages), they are indelibly part of the day-in and day-out workings of Hollywood even today. Production schedules are set based on the number of pages to be shot per day. Writers make decisions about whether or not to cut a scene based on their script's page count. An accurate page count is taken so seriously in Hollywood that senior executives at Warner Bros. once threatened to disband their own script processing department when they suspected its staff had compromised standard script margins on one critical draft of a feature film script. Altering a script's font or margins or even paper size from the standard changes the amount of material that fits on a page and thereby upsets all the calculations based on script page counts. It also changes the appearance of the page in ways that can instantly brand a script as unprofessional. Writers do so at their own peril.

A script page typed with standard margins looks like this:

1

[9]14.

[8]21   [2]EXT. BATTLEFIELD - DAWN   [8]21

[3]The sun rises crimson over the fallen soldiers.
Ragged children move among the dead, searching for
survivors. Or a serviceable pair of boots.

[5]UNION CAPTAIN
[4]You younguns, git!
[6](turning to his
men)
Ever' body knows his job. Let's
git to it!

The men start reluctantly across the field.

[7]CUT TO:

22   EXT. GRANT'S HEADQUARTERS - NIGHT   22

A fire burns outside a dirty canvas tent. Officers
mill. Everyone seems to be waiting for something to
happen.

Standard single-camera film format margins

Standard single-camera film format margins are as follows:

1. **Paper** is 3-hole punched 8 1/2" x 11" white 20 lb. bond.

2. **Shot headings:**
    Left margin is 1.7" (position 17)
    Right margin is 1.1" (position 73)
    Line length is 57 characters

3. **Direction:**
    Left margin is 1.7" (position 17)
    Right margin is 1.1" (position 73)
    Line length is 57 characters

4. **Dialogue:**
    Left margin is 2.7" (position 27)
    Right margin is 2.4" (position 60)
    Line length is 34 characters

5. **Character name over dialogue:**
    Left margin is 4.1" (position 41)
    Note that the character name over dialogue is not centered. It begins at the same fixed point (4.1" from the left edge of the page) no matter how long it is.

6. **Parenthetical character direction:**
    Left margin is 3.4" (position 34)
    Right margin is 3.1" (position 53)
    Line length is 19 characters

7. **Scene transitions:**
    Left margin is 6.0" (position 60)

8. **Scene numbers:**
    Left scene number goes 1.0" from the left edge of the page (position 10)
    Right scene number goes 7.4" from the left edge of the page (position 74)

9. **Page numbers:**
> Go at 7.2" (position 72), .5" below the top edge of the page.

10. **Font:**
> Courier or Courier New 12 point (or equivalent fixed-pitch serif font)

11. **Page length:**
> 60 lines (which allows for .5" margin at the top and bottom of each page)
>
> These 60 lines include one line at the top of each page for the page number, followed by a blank line and the text of the script.

Are script pages printed on one side of the page or two?

In an effort to save paper, some studios have experimented with double-sided script printing and some literary agencies routinely copy scripts on both sides of the page. Nevertheless, the longstanding practice in Hollywood has been to print scripts only on one side of the page. This makes reading the script far easier and provides room for the abundant notes that are regularly written on script pages. In addition, once a project approaches production, single-sided printing is an absolute necessity to make possible the replacement of individual script pages with colored revision pages.

SHOT HEADINGS

Also called *scene headings* and *slug lines*, shot headings can provide a wide variety of information about a given scene or shot. **They are always typed in capital letters.** They can be short and sweet:

        BOB

Or long and complicated:

        EXT. WHITE HOUSE - SOUTH LAWN - CLOSE ON CNN
        CORRESPONDENT - SUNSET (MARCH 15, 1999)

■ The five parts of a shot heading

Shot headings consist of up to five basic categories of information: 1) *interior* or *exterior*; 2) *location*; 3) *type of shot*; 4) *subject of shot*; and 5) *time of day*.

Interior or Exterior

A shot heading may begin with the abbreviation EXT., which stands for exterior. It tells us the scene takes place outdoors, a critical piece of information for anyone involved in production since most exterior scenes are shot outdoors rather than inside a sound stage.

The abbreviation INT. stands for interior and tells us the scene takes place indoors. Interior scenes are often shot on a stage.

INT. and EXT. are always capitalized and followed by a period and a single space, like this:

        INT. SPACE STATION

Not:

INT. SPACE STATION

Int. Space Station

INT: SPACE STATION

INT SPACE STATION

INT - SPACE STATION

Once in a while, a scene takes place both inside and outside. Let's say Molly, a sweet, ordinary girl, is locked in a battle with a wolverine while she's driving her Ferrari along the Hollywood Freeway and will be climbing onto the hood of her car during the shot. There are a couple of ways to set that up:

EXT. HOLLYWOOD FREEWAY/INT. MOLLY'S FERRARI - DAY

Steering with her bare feet, Molly hoists herself through the open window, wildly swinging her purse at the rabid wolverine.

Or:

EXT./INT. MOLLY'S FERRARI - DAY

Racing along the Hollywood Freeway. Steering with her feet, Molly hoists herself through the open window, wildly swinging her purse at the rabid wolverine.

Note that EXT./INT. contains a period after each abbreviation.

Sometimes writers are unsure whether a scene should be designated INT. or EXT. Our hero may have just climbed out of his car — after driving it into his garage. EXT. CAR isn't the correct designation because the scene is actually taking place inside the garage. Correct shot headings in this case include INT. GARAGE - OUTSIDE CAR or simply INT. GARAGE.

What if a scene is taking place inside an open-air stadium? It's still outdoors, so it's EXT.:

EXT. FENWAY PARK - UPPER DECK

Not:

     INT. FENWAY PARK - UPPER DECK

Just think "INT. for indoors" and "EXT. for outdoors" and you'll know what to do.

An important rule: **If you use a designation of INT. or EXT., you must always follow it immediately with a location:**

     EXT. GOLDEN GATE PARK - JACK

Not:

     EXT. JACK IN GOLDEN GATE PARK

     EXT. JACK

     EXT. DAY

     EXT. WIDE SHOT - JACK

Location

Location tells us where the scene takes place:

     EXT. SURFACE OF MOON - TRANQUILITY BASE

     INT. MUSTANG - TRUNK SPACE

     INT. HONOLULU HILTON - PRESIDENTIAL SUITE - BATHROOM

     EXT. FRED'S BACK YARD

An important rule: **A shot heading may contain just one location element or several, but those elements are always listed in order** *from general to specific*, **with each element separated by a hyphen (single space, hyphen, single space), like so:**

     EXT. LOS ANGELES - DOWNTOWN - BONAVENTURE HOTEL - LOADING DOCK

Not:

     INT. DRESSING ROOM - STARLET'S TRAILER
        (This one gets it backward, starting specific then going general.)

```
        CORN FIELD -- FARM -- IOWA
```
(Again, the order is backward, and the hyphens are wrong.)

```
        EXT. MANHATTAN STREET. SCENE OF CAR ACCIDENT. SOHO.
```
(The order here is scrambled and the hyphens have been replaced by periods.)

When an interior location includes a city name, put the city name in parentheses after the main location entry:

```
        INT. RAMSHACKLE WAREHOUSE (HONOLULU) - DAY

        INT. HOTEL ADLON (BERLIN) - 7TH FLOOR GUEST ROOM - NIGHT
```

Type of shot

Sometimes a writer wants to indicate a specific type of shot. There are many: establishing shots, wide shots, close shots, tracking shots, extreme closeups, insert shots, underwater shots, POV shots, and more. How frequently new shot headings should be inserted is a matter of much controversy and confusion. For now, we will list each type of shot and how each is properly formatted. Later, we will discuss some guidelines both practical and stylistic that will help writers decide when new shots should and should not be used.

• Closeup

A *closeup shot* indicates that the camera is focusing closely on a subject. Close shots can be set up in a variety of ways. Each of the following is correct:

```
        CLOSE - RUDOLPH'S NOSE

        CLOSE SHOT - RUDOLPH'S NOSE

        CLOSEUP - RUDOLPH'S NOSE

        CLOSE ON RUDOLPH'S NOSE

        CLOSE ANGLE ON RUDOLPH'S NOSE
```

Note that CLOSE, CLOSE SHOT and CLOSEUP are all followed by a hyphen, while CLOSE ON and CLOSE ANGLE ON are not. Note also that CLOSEUP is one word, not two.

• *Extreme closeup*

A variant of the closeup is the *extreme closeup*:

```
EXTREME CLOSEUP - IRIS OF WILLIAM'S LEFT EYE
```

• *Insert shot*

An *insert shot* is a special kind of closeup featuring a prop to show some important detail. Often an insert shot focuses on the written text of a sign, book, or note:

```
JOHN

rips the envelope and pulls out a birthday card.  He
opens it.

INSERT - CARD

Words scrawled in burgundy lipstick: "ENJOY YOUR
BIRTHDAY.  IT'S YOUR LAST."

BACK TO SCENE

John reacts with alarm.  He takes a closer look at
the envelope.
```

Note that after an insert shot, a new shot heading is necessary to bring us back into the main action. *Back to scene* is a useful, generic shot heading to accomplish that.

• *Wide shot*

A *wide shot* moves the camera away from the subject and takes in a swath of scenery. Wide shots can be set up in any of the following ways:

```
WIDE - RACETRACK AND EMPTY STANDS

WIDE SHOT - RACETRACK AND EMPTY STANDS

WIDE ANGLE - RACETRACK AND EMPTY STANDS

WIDE ON RACETRACK AND EMPTY STANDS

WIDE ANGLE ON RACETRACK AND EMPTY STANDS
```

As before, when the preposition "on" is used, a hyphen is not.

• *Medium shot*

Between the wide shot and the closeup is the *medium shot*, abbreviated MED. SHOT. Its subject is always one or more characters and it comes in only one flavor, like so:

```
MED. SHOT - JACK AND ROSE
```

Not:

```
MEDIUM SHOT - JACK AND ROSE
     (Don't spell out MEDIUM.)
```

```
MED. SHOT ON JACK AND ROSE
     (Don't use the preposition ON)
```

```
MED. - JACK AND ROSE
     (Don't omit the word SHOT)
```

• *Two and three shot*

A *two shot* is framed to feature two characters. A *three shot* features three characters:

```
TWO SHOT - BRUTUS AND CAESAR

THREE SHOT - MANNY, MOE AND JACK
```

Not:

```
BRUTUS AND CAESAR - TWO SHOT
     (The subject of the shot should follow the type of shot.)
```

```
THREE SHOT OF MANNY, MOE AND JACK
     (Use a hyphen instead of the word OF)
```

• *Establishing shot*

An *establishing shot* is used to show the exterior of a location, usually a building of some kind, inside which the next scene will take place. **In a true establishing shot, no action specific to the story takes place and no recognizable characters appear.** It is simply a shot that establishes the identity of the building we are about to go inside and the time of day. It can be set up like this:

```
EXT. BERTIE'S BREWHOUSE - ESTABLISHING SHOT - DAY

The parking lot is empty.

                                        CUT TO:

INT. BERTIE'S BREWHOUSE

Bertie mops the floor.
```

The following are also correct:

```
EXT. BERTIE'S BREWHOUSE - DAY

ESTABLISHING.  The parking lot is empty.


EXT. BERTIE'S BREWHOUSE - ESTABLISHING - DAY

EXT. BERTIE'S BREWHOUSE - DAY (ESTABLISHING)

EXT. BERTIE'S BREWHOUSE - TO ESTABLISH - DAY
```

Not:

```
EXT. BERTIE'S BREWHOUSE - ESTABLISHING - DAY

Bertie trudges outside and dumps a bucket of dirty
water.
```
> (If you have specific characters or action in the shot like we do here, it is not an establishing shot. Just drop the word "establishing" and you've got a perfectly formatted scene.)

• *Tracking and moving shot*

In a *tracking shot*, the camera moves with the action. Closely related is the *moving shot*. All of the following are correct:

```
TRACKING SHOT - MAN OF WAR

gallops down the back stretch, kicking up heavy
clumps of mud.
```

```
TRACKING SHOT

Man of War gallops down the back stretch, kicking up
heavy clumps of mud.

INT. MUSTANG CONVERTIBLE - MOVING - DAY

EXT. FIFTH AVENUE - MOVING SHOT - GRETA AND CURTIS

MOVING WITH PARADE FLOAT

TRACKING MAN OF WAR
```

Not:

```
MOVING WITH - PARADE FLOAT
```
(The preposition WITH eliminates the need for the hyphen.)

```
TRACKING - MAN OF WAR
```
(Either add the word SHOT after TRACKING or eliminate the hyphen.)

• *Aerial shot*

An *aerial shot* is photographed from the air:

```
AERIAL SHOT - BEACHES OF NORMANDY

EXT. BEACHES OF NORMANDY - AERIAL SHOT - D-DAY
```

• *Underwater shot*

An *underwater shot* can be formatted in a couple of different ways:

```
INT. GIANT AQUARIUM - MOVING WITH SHARK (UNDERWATER)
- DAY

UNDERWATER SHOT - DECK OF SUNKEN FREIGHTER
```

• *New angle*

Sometimes a writer may want to indicate a *new angle* within an existing scene without specifying exactly what sort of angle it is. These shot headings may be formatted as follows:

```
NEW ANGLE

NEW ANGLE - BALL FIELD

ANGLE - PANTING GOLDEN RETRIEVER

ANGLE ON SOPHIA
```

Sometimes ANGLE ON is shortened to just ON:

```
EXT. VENICE BEACH - ON SOPHIA - DAY

ON MIKE'S CLENCHED FIST
```

Note that ANGLE or NEW ANGLE should be used only within an existing scene, after a location has already been established. In other words, a scene that begins with the shot heading EXT. DODGERS STADIUM - DAY can later include the shot headings NEW ANGLE - SCOREBOARD and ANGLE ON UMPIRE, but not the shot headings NEW ANGLE - PORPOISES AT SEA or ANGLE ON HOLLYWOOD SIGN.

• *Up angle and down angle*

An *up angle* indicates that the camera is shooting upward, while a *down angle* indicates that the camera is shooting down toward its subject:

```
UP ANGLE - GOLIATH

DOWN ANGLE - TINY TIM
```

• *High angle and low angle*

A *high angle* indicates that the camera is placed up high, while a *low angle* indicates that the camera is placed down low:

```
HIGH ANGLE

HIGH ANGLE - LOOKING DOWN ON BATTLEFIELD

LOW ANGLE

LOW ANGLE - LOOKING UP TOWARD ROOFTOPS
```

• *Reverse angle*

A *reverse angle* is used to indicate that we have cut to a shot in which the camera is shooting in the opposite direction from the previous shot. It is used in a sequence like this one:

```
BATTER

swings his bat and connects with the baseball.

REVERSE ANGLE

The ball rockets past the pitcher into centerfield.
```

Here's another example:

```
INT. LIVING ROOM - CHRISTMAS MORNING

The little girl steps through the doorway and looks
into the room with delicious expectation.  But her
face instantly falls.

REVERSE ANGLE - CHRISTMAS TREE

Bare.  All the lights and ornaments are gone.  The
presents too.  Only a scrap of ribbon and a smashed
red bow remain on the floor.
```

• *POV shot*

The *POV shot* is an important one but is often incorrectly formatted in ways that confuse the reader. In a POV shot, the camera is looking through the eyes of a character, which allows the audience to see from that character's *point of view*. It is almost always part of a larger sequence of at least three shots: 1) the shot that shows the character looking at something; 2) the POV shot itself which shows what the character is seeing; and 3) a shot which returns to the main action of the scene. A typical sequence looks like this:

```
EXT. BANKS OF MISSISSIPPI RIVER - MORNING

Huck stares at something moving on the surface of
the water.
```

```
HUCK'S POV

A cottonmouth snake swims lazily toward him.

BACK TO SCENE

Huck picks up a rock and grins at the deadly reptile.
```

Also correct:

```
EXT. BANKS OF MISSISSIPPI RIVER - MORNING

Huck stares at something moving on the surface of
the water.

HUCK'S POV - COTTONMOUTH SNAKE

swims lazily toward him.

HUCK
```
(Here the word HUCK serves as an alternative to BACK TO SCENE.)

```
picks up a rock and grins at the deadly reptile.
```

Another older and rarely used — but entirely correct — formulation for a POV shot is WHAT HE SEES or WHAT HUCK SEES:

```
EXT. BANKS OF MISSISSIPPI RIVER - MORNING

Huck stares at something moving on the surface of
the water.

WHAT HE SEES

A cottonmouth snake swimming lazily toward him.

BACK TO HUCK
```
(BACK TO HUCK is another acceptable alternative to BACK TO SCENE.)

```
He picks up a rock and grins at the deadly reptile.
```

Here is an example of a common mistake:

```
        HUCK'S POV - COTTONMOUTH SNAKE
        swims lazily toward him.  He picks up a rock and
        grins at the deadly reptile.
```

This is incorrect because Huck can't appear in his own POV shot. An important rule: **Once we cut to a POV shot, we're looking directly through the character's eyes and he isn't going to see himself** (except in rare instances when he's seeing his reflection in a mirror, for example, or his image on a store's video monitor). Before we can see Huck, we have to cut to some new shot that includes him, most often Back To Scene or Back To Huck.

Another common and confusing mistake:

```
        POV - HUCK
```

Is this Huck's POV, meaning that we're looking through Huck's eyes? Or is this someone else's POV looking at Huck? It's impossible to tell, which is why it's a mistake.

Sometimes a writer wants to call for a POV shot without revealing yet whose POV it is in order to maintain mystery. Here's an example of how to set that up:

```
        EXT. DARK PARKING LOT - NIGHT

        Rita climbs from her Miata.

        MYSTERY POV

        Watching FROM BEHIND bushes as she walks alone
        toward the lake.
```

Also correct:

```
        WATCHER'S POV

        ANONYMOUS POV

        SUBJECTIVE CAMERA
```

Subjective camera is simply another way of indicating that the camera is looking through a character's eyes.

Specialized types of POV shots include binocular POVs, microscopic POVs, upside-down POVs, and POV shots out windows and through sniper scopes. They can be formatted as follows:

```
BINOCULAR POV

SGT. GRIGGS' BINOCULAR POV - ENEMY INFANTRYMEN

move along the distant ridge.

MICROSCOPIC POV

The bacterium slowly divides, then divides again.

PETER'S UPSIDE-DOWN POV - DANCE FLOOR

Everyone seems to be dancing on the ceiling.

PAMELA'S POV - THROUGH WINDOW

Rain has begun to fall.

POV SHOT THROUGH SNIPER SCOPE - PRIME MINISTER

The cross hairs hover over the official.
```

• *Handheld shot*

A *handheld shot* is one in which the camera is being held by the camera operator to give an added sense of motion, energy, or confusion, or to heighten the illusion that we're seeing through a character's eyes in a POV shot:

```
HANDHELD SHOT - MOVING WITH MURPHY

As he runs for his life, breathing hard, sweating
like an iced tea on an August day in Georgia.
```

Also correct:

```
MOVING WITH MURPHY (HANDHELD)
```

Subject of shot

Separate from the type of shot is the *subject of the shot*, meaning the character or object being featured in the shot. The subject is a thing, something concrete and visible. It may be as small as a couple of mice or as enormous as a mountain range:

```
MICKEY AND MINNEY

HIMALAYAS
```

It may include descriptors:

```
CRYING BOY AND HIS SNIFFLING LITTLE SISTER

LAST MAN ON EARTH
```

But no element of a shot heading should include action. The following are incorrect:

```
SLEEPY BOY RUBS HIS EYES

NAVY SEALS CREEP UP BEACH
```

Instead, separate the subject of the shot from the action, like this:

```
SLEEPY BOY

rubs his eyes.

NAVY SEALS

creep up the beach.
```

If a shot has more than one subject, separate the multiple subjects with commas, slashes, or the conjunction "and":

```
TRACKING SHOT - MIKE, SAMMY, SAL AND WANDA

THREE SHOT - HANSEL/GRETEL/WITCH

SERGEANT AND TWO CORPORALS

WIDE SHOT - TEX GRIFFIN, HIS PONY AND STONY RIDGE
BEYOND THEM
```

Not:

```
WIDE SHOT - TEX GRIFFIN - HIS PONY - STONY RIDGE
BEYOND THEM
```

Time of Day

A shot heading often indicates what *time of day* a scene is taking place. The most basic designations are Day and Night, and they're important not only for maintaining a reader's orientation within the story but also because they have important practical implications for production.

Day indicates that a scene takes place during daylight.

Night indicates that a scene takes place in the dark.

Magic hour is used to describe the very short period at sunset when the light is waning but the sun has not yet set. It's called magic because it makes for great pictures, but it's also terribly short and so it isn't practical to shoot long scenes under these brief conditions.

Sunset, sunrise, and *dusk* are all acceptable designations, but also carry practical limitations for production.

Writers may also indicate a time of day more specifically or colorfully:

```
DEAD OF NIGHT

HIGH NOON

3 AM
```

Other time designations help the reader remain oriented within time, especially when a screenplay's narrative is nonlinear, meaning it doesn't unfold in strictly chronological order:

```
INT. BEDROOM - ON SLEEPING CHILD - 15 MINUTES LATER

EXT. SWIMMING POOL - CONTINUOUS ACTION

EXT. INDEPENDENCE HALL - JULY 4, 1776

EXT. WHITE HOUSE - ESTABLISHING - PRESENT DAY

INT. PENTICUFF HOUSE - GARAGE - FIVE MONTHS EARLIER

INT. SUBWAY CAR - SAME TIME
```

Occasionally, more than one time descriptor is used in a single shot heading. In such cases, **the term that actually describes the time of day comes first, followed in parentheses by the additional modifiers:**

```
EXT. MOGADISHU - WEAPONS MARKET - DAY (AUGUST 5, 1995)

INT. CLASSROOM - NIGHT (CONTINUOUS ACTION)

EXT. BMW DEALERSHIP - SUNRISE (BACK TO PRESENT)
```

The term *Continuous Action* is used to indicate that one scene follows the preceding one immediately, without any intervening passage of time:

```
INT. HALLWAY

Running for her life, Penelope bangs up against the
door and twists the knob.

INT. DOCTOR'S OFFICE WAITING ROOM - CONTINUOUS ACTION

Her eyes wild, Penelope stumbles inside, desperate
to find a friendly face.
```

CONTINUOUS ACTION can sometimes be useful to make clear to the reader that no time has passed between shots or scenes, but it is often overused. In the example above, context makes fairly obvious that the action from one shot to the next is continuous. The use of CONTINUOUS ACTION adds little. It simply clutters the page with unnecessary words. A cleaner, crisper style results when CONTINUOUS ACTION is used sparingly and only when added clarity is required.

Various additional descriptors are also lumped into the "time of day" category, even though they have nothing to do with the actual time of day. They include terms describing weather (*rain, snow, sleet,* etc.), the quality of the film or video stock being used (*black and white, 8 mm, home video, newsreel footage,* etc.), *slow motion,* and *MOS,* an old Hollywood term with an amusing history. MOS indicates a scene filmed without sound. Hollywood folklore holds that this term arose from German directors working in early Hollywood who in their limited English would order a scene shot "mit-out sound," duly noted on the script as "MOS."

```
EXT. DISNEYLAND - NEAR SPLASH MOUNTAIN - DAY (HOME
VIDEO)
```

```
EXT. DALLAS BOOK DESPOSITORY - ON JFK IN OPEN
CONVERTIBLE - DAY (BLACK AND WHITE)

INT. THEATER - ON STAGE - NIGHT (MOS)
```

The actors go through their motions. Mouths move appropriately. Singers sing. Dancers dance. But we hear nothing of it. Only the disembodied PLINK, PLINK, PLINK of a TOY PIANO coming from who knows where.

```
EXT. CENTRAL PARK - CHRISTMAS NIGHT (SNOW)

INT. ORIENT EXPRESS - DAY (RAIN)

EXT. CHICAGO WORLD'S FAIR - DAY (NEWSREEL FOOTAGE)

CLOSE ON BULLET (SLOW MOTION)

EXT. RACE TRACK - AIRBORNE STOCK CAR - DAY (SLOW
MOTION)

CHILD'S BIRTHDAY PARTY - DAY (1966) (8MM)
```

Note in the examples above that the term describing the actual time of day comes first, followed by the additional modifier or modifiers in parentheses.

■ How to arrange the information in a shot heading

As we've seen, a shot heading can contain information in up to five distinct categories: 1) interior or exterior; 2) location; 3) type of shot; 4) subject of shot; and 5) time of day. **The information should be presented in exactly that order.**

```
[1]INT. [2]FUNHOUSE - [3]MED. SHOT - [4]MR. WHIPPLE - [5]NIGHT
```

Very long shot headings are possible that contain a relatively large amount of information in each of the five of categories:

```
[1]INT. [2]FUNHOUSE - COLLAPSING REAR SECTION - HALL OF
MIRRORS - [3]SLOW TRACKING SHOT - [4]MR. WHIPPLE, MRS.
WHIPPLE AND YOUNG WINSTEAD WHIPPLE - [5]NIGHT
(CONTINUOUS ACTION) (BLACK AND WHITE)
```

But notice that even in this unnaturally long and ungainly shot heading, the information is laid out according to the same simple plan.

Of course many shot headings contain information from only one or a few of the five possible categories. Here, the rule is the same. Simply lay out what you have in the established order:

```
¹INT. ²FUNHOUSE - ⁵NIGHT

³MED. SHOT - ⁴MR. WHIPPLE

⁴WHIPPLE
```

■ How to decide what information to include in shot headings

Writers sometimes wonder how much information should be included in shot headings. Many writers include too much information, much of it redundant, making the screenplay cluttered and difficult to read. Other writers fail to provide enough information, which can leave the reader confused. **The goal when composing a shot heading should be to provide the necessary information clearly and concisely, including just enough words to do the job but no more.** Here are three general guidelines to help you decide how much information is enough, and which will go a great distance toward reducing the length of your shot headings:

1.   **At the beginning of a sequence that takes place in a new location or after a passage of time, indicate INT. or EXT. and a description of the location, along with an indication of the time of day:**

```
INT. WHITE HOUSE - OVAL OFFICE - DAY
```

These are often called *master shot headings.*

2.   **If specific shots follow a master shot heading and occur in the same location and within the same time frame, it isn't necessary to repeat the location and time of day.**

The master shot heading above could be followed by shots like these:

```
ANGLE ON PRESIDENT'S DESK

MED. SHOT - PRESIDENT BARTLETT

LEO
```

3.   **Shot headings should be as short as possible.**

In general, the readability of a script increases as the word count decreases. That's why rule #2 above is important. Endlessly repeating something like INT. WHITE HOUSE - OVAL OFFICE as part of each of the minor shot headings turns a simple thing like LEO into the jawbreaker INT. WHITE HOUSE - OVAL OFFICE - LEO - DAY. Not only is this shot heading far more work to read, it obscures the most important element in the shot – Leo. It also breaks up the continuity of the ongoing master scene and suggests that a time cut may have occurred. All of this slows, confuses, and potentially irritates the busy reader.

Information about the type of shot can also frequently be omitted. Rarely is it necessary to indicate FULL SHOT - LEO or MED. SHOT - LEO, rather than simply LEO. When it is necessary to the telling of the story to call a specific type of shot, such as a POV shot or a close shot, by all means do it. But **when there is no strongly compelling reason to specify a particular type of shot, don't.** Leave it to the director.

■ How to decide when to create a new shot heading

Including too many shot headings or too few often creates problems for writers and readers alike. Too many shot headings clutter a screenplay and can make a writer appear amateurish. Too few shot headings leave the reader confused and create headaches when production approaches. **In general, insert a new shot heading only when necessary.** Three rules of thumb provide guidance here:

1.   **Insert a shot heading when there is a change in location or time.**

Let's say we're inside the Oval Office (INT. OVAL OFFICE - DAY), and then cut outside to the Lincoln Memorial. We would need a new shot heading along these lines: EXT. LINCOLN MEMORIAL - DAY. That's fairly straightforward.

Now let's say we're in the Oval Office, then we cut to another scene in the same location, but it's 90 minutes later. We need a new shot heading, something like this: INT. OVAL OFFICE - 90 MINUTES LATER or SAME - 90 MINUTES LATER.

Writers sometimes get into trouble when a character moves from one location to another. The following is incorrect:

```
INT. JOSIAH'S MOTOR HOME - NIGHT

The old guy pours himself a cup of coffee and
steps outside.  He climbs painfully to the
ground and looks up at the stars.
```

We're missing a shot heading that accounts for Josiah's movement from an interior location to an exterior one, which may be shot at a completely different time and place. The sequence should be set up like this:

```
INT. JOSIAH' MOTOR HOME - NIGHT

The old guys pours himself a cup of coffee and
steps outside.

EXT. MOTOR HOME - NIGHT

He climbs painfully to the ground and looks up
at the stars.
```

2.   **Add shot headings when necessary for the visual telling of the story.**

Among the screenwriter's tasks is creating the visual experience of the screen story in the imagination of the reader. Shot headings are one of the essential tools for accomplishing this task. We have already discussed what many of these shots are: POV shots, close shots, wide shots, tracking shots, up angles, down angles, and so forth. If visual attention must be focused very specifically on a small object or detail, an extreme close shot serves precisely that purpose and is appropriate and justified. At other times, say in an ordinary dialogue scene between two characters, it might not be necessary to call attention to any particular visual detail and only the initial master shot heading is required. Add shot headings of the more visually specific sort only when you have a compelling visual reason for doing so.

3.   **Add shot headings when logic requires it.**

Sometimes plain logic requires a new shot heading. For example, after the shot heading WILMA'S POV, a new shot heading, such as BACK TO SCENE, is logically required before Wilma can appear again on screen. Similarly, after an EXTREME CLOSEUP ON GNAT'S LITTLE TOE, logic requires a new shot heading before the expanse of the Grand Canyon may appear on screen.

4.   **Don't add a shot heading where there is no new shot.**

Sometimes writers set up as a shot heading what is really just a movement of the camera. The following is incorrect:

```
INT. SUBMARINE - GALLEY - NIGHT

Nason and his guys fight the fire.  They know
that at this depth, they're fighting for their
lives.  But they're choking on the smoke.  And
they're losing the battle.

PAN TO ENSIGN MENENDEZ

Leading in a fresh contingent of men to join
the fight.
```

The pan is really just a camera move within the existing shot and shouldn't logically be given a new shot heading. Instead, format the sequence like this:

```
INT. SUBMARINE - GALLEY - NIGHT

Nason and his guys fight the fire.  They know
that at this depth, they're fighting for their
lives.  But they're choking on the smoke.  And
they're losing the battle.  PAN TO Ensign
Menendez, leading in a fresh contingent of men
to join the fight.
```

Other common camera moves that don't logically warrant new shot headings include RACK FOCUS TO, TILT or PAN TO REVEAL and ZOOM or TRACK TO.

An important exception to this rule occurs when we start on a closeup or an extreme closeup and pull back to reveal that we're in a whole new location. For practical reasons (namely, that production personnel need a new master shot heading to go with the new location), a new shot heading is added.

Instead of this:

```
EXTREME CLOSEUP - WOMAN'S FIST
```

```
         opens to show she holds a house key.  She
         inserts it in a doorknob.  PULL BACK to reveal
         Dotty opening the front door of Frank's house.
         Dotty lets herself in.
```

Do this:

```
         EXTREME CLOSEUP - WOMAN'S FIST

         opens to show she holds a house key.  She
         inserts it in a doorknob.  PULL BACK to reveal:

         EXT. FRANK'S HOUSE

         Dotty opens the front door and lets herself in.
```

5. **Add shot headings to break up long passages of action and lend a sense of increased tempo.**

The problem: Because of the narrow column that even intermittent dialogue makes down the center of the script page, a screenplay often contains a great deal of white space. Add in the space around shot headings, scene transitions and a few short paragraphs, and a typical script page contains relatively few words, looks spacious and reads fairly breezily. By contrast, action sequences, arguably the fastest-paced sequences written for the screen, can appear in a script like dull blocks of words crowding the page. Ironically, then, when an action sequence obliterates too much of the white space, action can end up reading so slowly that readers are tempted to skim it or even skip it entirely.

The solution: Break up the action with short shot headings to restore white space and help guide the reader's eye down the page. Compare the following sequences, the first with only a single master shot heading and the second with additional shot headings inserted to break up the page.

```
         INT. PARKING STRUCTURE - DAY

         The immaculate MOTOR HOME ROARS down the ramp
         into the underground garage, followed by three
         squad cars.  Michael cranks the steering wheel
         hard to the right and the MOTOR HOME makes a
         SQUEALING turn.  Ahead, a concrete beam hangs
         low.  Too low for the high-profile vehicle.
         Michael ducks at the moment of IMPACT.  The ROOF
         PEELS OFF the motor home with a METALLIC SHRIEK.
```

The crumpled SHEET METAL BANGS off the hood of a pursuing squad car. One of the cops slings a RIOT GUN out his window and FIRES. The GLASS in Michael's WINDOW EXPLODES. He makes a desperation left turn down another ramp but cuts the corner too close. A long slab of METAL CURLS AWAY from the side of the motor home like an orange peel. Michael plunges his giant convertible deeper into the garage, his hair blowing in the open air. At the bottom of the ramp, steel pipes crisscross the low ceiling. What's left of the MOTOR HOME GRINDS against them and debris flies as the big vehicle gets chopped down even shorter. Shreds of insulation, stuffed animals and cooking utensils fill the air. A microwave oven bounces onto the hood of a squad car and SMASHES THROUGH the WINDSHIELD, landing in the empty passenger seat. Michael finds a ramp sloping up toward daylight and heads for freedom, no longer pursued, piloting the decimated chassis of what was once his proud home.

While this might be fun to watch on screen, it looks fairly awful on the page. Here is the same action broken up with intermediate shot headings that correspond roughly to the various smaller pieces of action that make up the whole sequence:

INT. PARKING STRUCTURE - DAY

The immaculate MOTOR HOME ROARS down the ramp into the underground garage, followed by three squad cars.

MICHAEL

cranks the steering wheel hard to the right and:

MOTOR HOME

makes a SQUEALING turn. Ahead, a concrete beam hangs low. Too low for the high-profile vehicle.

Occasionally, omitting an article causes a shot heading to read awkwardly. In those cases, it is acceptable to include the article.

■ Formatting specialized sequences

Certain specialized sequences, such as flashbacks, dream sequences, split screens, and telephone intercuts, require special treatment.

Flashbacks and dream sequences

A *flashback* is a scene or series of scenes that takes place prior to the story's main action. A *dream sequence* is, naturally, a scene or series of scenes that takes place in a dream. **In a flashback, the word "flashback" appears underlined as the very first element in the shot heading, followed by a hyphen:**

```
FLASHBACK - INT. FUNHOUSE - NIGHT
```

A dream sequence is set up the same way:

```
DREAM SEQUENCE - INT. FUNHOUSE - NIGHT
```

Alternative, more recent terms sometimes used to introduce short flashbacks are *memory hit* and *memory flash*:

```
MEMORY HIT - CORVETTE

careens out of control.

MEMORY FLASH

Melissa's face the instant before impact.
```

Imagination sequences can be handled like dream sequences:

```
IAN'S IMAGINATION - INT. CIRCUS TENT
```

Ending a flashback or dream sequence

When a flashback or dream sequence ends, you have three choices. You can simply move on to the next scene:

DREAM SEQUENCE - EXT. FERRIS WHEEL - DAY

Josh dangles by his fingertips from the highest car.
Melanie sits in the car above him, prying his
fingers loose one by one. And suddenly, Josh is
falling, falling, falling...

INT. SCIENCE CLASSROOM - DAY

Josh jerks his head up off his desk, jolting awake.
He looks across the room at Melanie with deep
suspicion.

Here, the context makes obvious that the dream has ended and no further
formatting cues are required. Other less obvious situations benefit from a more
explicit indication that the flashback or dream is over. This is the second method
of ending a flashback or dream sequence:

DREAM SEQUENCE - EXT. FERRIS WHEEL - DAY

Josh dangles by his fingertips from the highest car.
Melanie sits in the car above him, prying his
fingers loose one by one. And suddenly, Josh is
falling, falling, falling...

                                        END DREAM SEQUENCE.

INT. SCIENCE CLASSROOM - DAY

Melanie looks up from her book and notices that Josh
is looking at her sort of cock-eyed, like he's just
woken up. He appears deeply, darkly suspicious.

A flashback can also be handled this same way:

FLASHBACK - EXT. RIVERBANK

Charity stands watching the big riverboat burn, her
hands over her mouth. Slowly she collapses in the
mud.

EXT. SMALL-TOWN CEMETERY

A half-dozen funerals underway simultaneously. The scope of the tragedy hits home. Charity stands at a fresh grave, grieving her sister alone.

END FLASHBACK.

INT. CHARITY'S BEDROOM - NIGHT

She stares at her image in the mirror.

A third way to indicate that a flashback has ended is to add the words BACK TO PRESENT to the shot heading that immediately follows the flashback:

FLASHBACK - EXT. RIVERBANK

Charity stands watching the big riverboat burn, her hands over her mouth. Slowly she collapses in the mud.

EXT. SMALL-TOWN CEMETERY

A half-dozen funerals underway simultaneously. The scope of the tragedy hits home. Charity stands at a fresh grave, grieving her sister alone.

INT. CHARITY'S BEDROOM - NIGHT (BACK TO PRESENT)

She stares at her image in the mirror.

Note that FLASHBACK is one word and that it appears only once, as does DREAM SEQUENCE, at the beginning of the sequence, even if the sequence consists of multiple scenes.

Montages and series of shots

A *montage* is a series of brief images, often under music, used to show the passage of time, the unfolding of a character's plan or the evolution of a character or relationship over time. A *series of shots* performs a similar function. Though purists will argue that there is an important difference between the two, that argument is beyond the scope of this guide. From a formatting standpoint, they are twins.

A montage includes the word MONTAGE in the shot heading. A series of shots includes the words SERIES OF SHOTS in the heading.

In either case, the shot heading is followed by a description of the content of the various shots that make up the montage or series of shots. Here is a montage:

```
AROUND PARIS - MONTAGE

Jim and Angela sit at a café, sipping coffee,
tentative with one another.

They walk through the Musee D'Orsay, pausing in
front of a Van Gogh, lost in animated conversation.
They seem surprised at what they're discovering in
each other.

They climb the endless iron stairs of the Eiffel
Tower. She's getting tired. He offers his hand.
She takes it and he pulls her along.

They stand on the Pont Neuf, gazing together at the
waters of the Seine flowing beneath them. The sun
is setting. Angela looks into Jim's eyes. She goes
up on her toes and gives him a tender first kiss.
```

Here is a series of shots:

```
SERIES OF SHOTS

John ransacks the glove compartment of the old
Dodge. He comes out with a book of matches.

He searches and finds a newspaper in a pile of trash
behind the house.

He rips the paper and crumples it into tight balls.

He stuffs the paper in the dark space beneath the house.

He strikes a match and sets fire to the crumpled
paper.

He sits in the Dodge, watching the house burn.
```

Each paragraph represents a shot within the montage or series of shots. This is the simplest formatting method. An alternative is to assign each shot within the montage or series of shots its own shot heading. The shots are then lettered alphabetically and the individual shot headings and descriptions are indented three spaces from the normal left margin:

```
AROUND PARIS - MONTAGE

A) EXT. CAFÉ - DAY

   Jim and Angela sit sipping coffee, tentative with
   one another.

B) INT. MUSEE D'ORSAY - DAY

   They walk through the museum, pausing in front of
   a Van Gogh, lost in animated conversation.  They
   seem surprised at what they're discovering in
   each other.

C) EXT. EIFFEL TOWER - DAY

   They climb the endless iron stairs of the Eiffel
   Tower.  She's getting tired.  He offers his hand.
   She takes it and he pulls her along.

D) EXT. SEINE RIVER - DUSK

   They stand on the Pont Neuf, gazing together at
   the waters of the Seine flowing beneath them.
   The sun is setting.  Angela looks into Jim's
   eyes.  She goes up on her toes and gives him a
   tender first kiss.
```

Both of these methods make clear what is the content of each individual shot, and which shots are included in the montage or series of shots, and there is no confusion about where the montage or series of shots ends.

Intercut sequences

An *intercut sequence* is one that cuts alternately between two or more locations, most often to present all parties to a telephone conversation. Each location must be established with its own shot heading, and the instruction INTERCUT must be given. Thereafter, dialogue can flow as if all the characters are present together and (V.O.) is not indicated beside any of the character names over dialogue:

INT. MARYANN'S KITCHEN - MORNING

She dials the phone.

INT. MARK'S OFFICE - SAME TIME

His PHONE begins to RING. He crosses to pick it up.

> MARK
> Mark Markisian and Associates.

INTERCUT telephone conversation.

> MARYANN
> Mark? It's Maryann. How are you?

> MARK
> Fantastic. I'm so glad you called.
> The messenger just brought your
> cashier's check.

Here is another way to format the same conversation:

INT. MARYANN'S KITCHEN - MORNING

She dials the phone. INTERCUT WITH:

INT. MARK'S OFFICE - SAME TIME

His PHONE begins to RING. He crosses to pick it up.

> MARK
> Mark Markisian and Associates.

> MARYANN
> Mark? It's Maryann. How are you?

> MARK
> Fantastic. I'm so glad you called.
> The messenger just brought your
> cashier's check.

Split screen sequences

A *split screen sequence* consists of two or more scenes simultaneously sharing the screen, which may be split into left and right halves, or four quadrants, or an entire checkerboard of smaller images. A two-location split screen gets a shot heading like this:

```
INT. GAS STATION BATHROOM/INT. FIFTH AVENUE LAW
OFFICE - SPLIT SCREEN - DAY

Milo, dressed in nothing but his boxers, has his
cell phone out and is waving it around the filthy
john, trying desperately to get a signal.  Back at
the office, his entire staff is searching just as
desperately for the missing report.
```

■ Capitalizing McDonald's and DeVries in shot headings

When names like McDonald's and DeVries appear in a shot heading, capitalize like this for greater readability:

```
INT. McDONALD'S RESTAURANT - CLOSE ON DeVRIES
```
   (The c in McDonald's and the e in DeVries are lower-cased.)

■ Breaking a page after a shot heading

Never break a page immediately after a shot heading. Always include at least one complete sentence of direction or one line of dialogue before breaking the page:

```
EXT. MOTOCROSS COURSE - DAY

The BIKES ROAR past.
-----page break -----
A cloud of dust fills the air in their wake.
```

An exception to this rule occurs when a shot heading stands alone as a scene:

```
EXT. McGREGOR MANSION - NIGHT (ESTABLISHING SHOT)
-----page break-----
INT. McGREGOR MANSION - NIGHT

The party is in progress.
```

■ Spacing between shots and scenes

Standard practice allows for either double spacing (one blank line) or triple spacing (two blank lines) before each new shot heading. You can do it like this:

```
EXT. COFFEE SHOP - DAY

Mick and Minn walk in.

INT. COFFEE SHOP - DAY

They sit down.
```

Or like this:

```
EXT. COFFEE SHOP - DAY

Mick and Minn walk in.


INT. COFFEE SHOP - DAY

They sit down.
```

The first method allows more material to fit on the page. The second method leaves more white space and looks more inviting to the reader.

A third method triple spaces before master scene headings and double spaces before each new shot heading within a master scene:

```
INT. COFFEE SHOP - DAY

They sit down.  Mick notices something on the table.

INSERT - TABLETOP

Something scratched into the finish.  The letters X,
G and Z.

BACK TO SCENE

He frowns.  Jots the letters on a napkin.
```

EXT. COFFEE SHOP

Mick runs for his car.

INT. POLICE PRECINCT

Mick strides in.

■ A rogues' gallery of nonstandard shot headings

All of the following shot headings are out of standard format. After each heading, an explanation of the problem is given, along with a corrected version of the shot heading:

EXT. MERCEDES - INTERSTATE 70
    (Follow the general-to-specific rule:
    EXT. INTERSTATE 70 - MERCEDES.)

EXT. APARTMENT - SPRING - 1965 - DAWN
    (You only get one main time-of-day designation, with the others following in parentheses:
    EXT. APARTMENT - DAWN (SPRING 1965).)

INT. TENEMENT APARTMENT - DETROIT - NIGHT
    (The city name should be placed inside parentheses: INT. TENEMENT APARTMENT (DETROIT) - NIGHT.)

INT. PLAYBOY MANSION/KITCHEN - DAY
    (As you move from general to specific, separate the location elements with a hyphen:
    INT. PLAYBOY MANSION - KITCHEN - DAY.)

EXT. THE FRONT OF THE BAR
    (Omit the articles: EXT. FRONT OF BAR.)

ANGLE ON BLENDER SPINNING AND SPINNING
    (Remove the action from the shot heading: ANGLE ON BLENDER, with "Spinning and spinning" placed beneath the shot heading in direction.)

MONTAGE
    (Only flashbacks and dream sequences get underlined: MONTAGE.)

CLOSE ON: ASTRONAUT JOHN GLENN
(Lose the colon: CLOSE ON ASTRONAUT JOHN GLENN.)

Angle on:

Mike lifting the heavy beam off Otto.
(Ouch. Do it like this: ANGLE ON MIKE, with "Lifting the heavy beam off Otto placed beneath the shot heading in direction".)

EXT. LAUNCH PAD -- SPACE SHUTTLE ENDEAVOR --
CONTINUOUS
(Separate the elements with a single hyphen (space hyphen space), not a dash: EXT. LAUNCH PAD - SPACE SHUTTLE ENDEAVOR - CONTINUOUS.)

I./E. MOLLY'S VW - DAY
(Spell it out: INT./EXT. MOLLY'S VW - DAY.)

INT. - PHONE BOOTH - MOMENTS LATER
(There's no hyphen after Int. or Ext.:
INT. PHONE BOOTH - MOMENTS LATER.)

EXT. PHIL'S APARTMENT - HALLWAY
(The hallway is really an interior location which happens to be outside Phil's apartment: INT. HALLWAY - OUTSIDE PHIL'S APARTMENT.)

A LONG STRETCH OF DESERT HIGHWAY - ARIZONA DESERT -
NOON
(Lose the article "A" and put the location in order from general to specific: EXT. ARIZONA DESERT - LONG STRETCH OF DESERT HIGHWAY - NOON.)

INT. - MED. SHOT - BECKMAN - DAY
(An INT. or EXT. designation requires a location: INT. RESTAURANT - MED. SHOT - BECKMAN - DAY.)

A LOUD BANG
(Sounds don't belong in shot headings. You can't photograph a loud bang. What do we see?)

EXT. DOWNTOWN CHICAGO - A HOT JULY AFTERNOON - MUSIC
OVER
> (Lose the article "A" and drop the "MUSIC OVER" down into
> direction beneath the shot heading: EXT. DOWNTOWN
> CHICAGO - HOT JULY AFTERNOON.)

CLOSE - ON YOUNG ENGLISH BOY
> (Don't put a hyphen between CLOSE and ON: CLOSE ON
> YOUNG ENGLISH BOY.)

INT. BASEMENT, VICTOR'S PLACE
> (The location always reads from general to specific and its parts
> are separated by hyphens: INT. VICTOR'S PLACE -
> BASEMENT.)

MED. SHOT
> (Of what? MED. SHOT - BRONCO BILLY.)

INT. EXTREME WIDE ANGLE - LIVING ROOM - DAY
> (Follow the established order of shot heading elements: INT.
> LIVING ROOM - EXTREME WIDE ANGLE - DAY.)

REVERSE ANGLE - EXT. COW PASTURE
> (Again, follow the established order: EXT. COW PASTURE -
> REVERSE ANGLE.)

DIRECTION

Also called *action* and *description*, direction consists of passages that describe what is being seen and heard within the shot or scene. It may include *introductions* and *descriptions of characters*, description of characters' actions and demeanor, *sounds* and *sound effects*, *visual effects* and *camera direction*. In short, direction tells us what's happening.

Direction is always written in the present tense:

```
Lydia leaps from the precipice and free-falls down
the cliff face, counting seven agonizing seconds
before pulling the rip chord.  A second later, the
yellow canopy blossoms above her.
```

Not:

```
Lydia leapt from the precipice and free-fell down
the cliff face, counting seven agonizing seconds
before pulling the rip chord.  A second later, the
yellow canopy blossomed above her.
```

Direction also tends to be written in relatively short, direct sentences designed to paint pictures using the fewest possible words.

■ Paragraphing in direction

All of the direction beneath a shot heading may be kept together in a single paragraph:

```
Lydia hits the ground and rolls.  She's immediately
jerked back to her feet as the canopy is caught in
the wind.  She fights to free herself from the
canopy.  She pulls a knife and slashes at its cords.
Something moves in the brush behind her.  Lydia cuts
herself free and the canopy blows away in the wind.
She turns toward the brush, the knife in front of
her.
```

Or it may be broken into several smaller paragraphs:

```
Lydia hits the ground and rolls.  She's immediately
jerked back to her feet as the canopy is caught in
the wind.

Lydia fights to free herself from the canopy.  She
pulls a knife and slashes at its cords.

Something moves in the brush behind her.

Lydia cuts herself free and the canopy blows away in
the wind.  She turns toward the brush, the knife in
front of her.
```

The advantages of breaking large passages of direction into smaller paragraphs are that it makes the text more readable, increases the reader's sense of pace and creates white space that helps the page look less dense and imposing. A further important advantage is that skillful and judicious use of paragraphing in direction allows the writer to direct the reader's visual imagination without resorting to a large number of shot headings. Notice how a sequence of specific visuals can be implied without adding individual shot headings:

```
Billy unlatches the tackle box and looks inside.

His finger sweeps aside a tangle of lures and
knotted fishing line to uncover the missing penny.

A look of wonder spreads over Billy's face.
```

The disadvantage to this style is that it takes more space, increasing the page count of the script (though not as much as does breaking the scene with additional shot headings). An effective screenwriting style balances these often competing considerations.

Paragraphs of direction are never indented:

```
Lydia hits the ground and rolls.  She's immediately
jerked back to her feet as the canopy is caught in
the wind.
```

■ Breaking a page in the middle of direction

Never break a page in the middle of a sentence in direction. When breaking direction, always split the page between sentences:

```
EXT. MOTOCROSS COURSE - DAY

The BIKES ROAR past.
-----page break -----
A cloud of dust fills the air in their wake.
```

Not:

```
EXT. MOTOCROSS COURSE - DAY

The BIKES ROAR past.  A cloud of dust fills the air in
-----page break -----
their wake.
```

■ Capitalization in direction

Standard script format dictates that words in direction are typed in all capital letters if they're performing one of only three tasks: 1) *introducing a speaking character*; 2) *describing sound effects and offscreen sounds*; or 3) *describing camera direction.*

```
[1]MACK HUMPHREYS runs through the door.  [2]FLAMES ROAR
all around him.  [3]CAMERA PUSHES IN CLOSE ON his
terrified face.
```

Introducing a speaking character

The first time a speaking character appears on screen, the character's name is typed in all capitals:

```
Dressed in his full space suit, JOHN GLENN steps out
of the launch tower elevator.  Launch workers
surround Glenn and help him toward the waiting
spacecraft.
```

Note in the example above that the second time Glenn's name appears, it is not typed in all capitals. **Each speaking character's name should be typed in all capitals once and only once.**

Even if a speaking character's name isn't a proper name, it still gets capitalized when the character first appears. Subsequently the first letter of the character name gets capitalized every time it appears:

```
A stunning BALLERINA steps before the stage lights.
The Ballerina curtseys and begins to dance.
```

Many times, a character will be described somewhat generically, as a "woman" or a "firefighter," before her name appears in direction. As long as the proper name appears fairly quickly after the generic reference, wait and capitalize just the proper name:

```
A firefighter runs through the door.  Her name is
LORI HEDDEN.  The fire burns hot all around her.
She's terrified.
```

However, if the firefighter speaks before we know her name, we have no choice but to capitalize the word "firefighter" and then, later, her proper name once we learn it:

```
A FIREFIGHTER runs through the door.

                         FIREFIGHTER
               Anybody in here?

The fire burns hot all around her.  She's terrified.
Her name is LORI HEDDEN.

                         LORI (FIREFIGHTER)
               Anybody? !
```

Don't be fooled by a character name that shows up before the character does. Wait to capitalize the name until the character himself appears onscreen:

```
Launch workers gather around the tower elevator,
waiting for John Glenn to emerge.  The door slides
to the side and GLENN steps out in his full space
suit.
```

If a speaking character first appears in a shot heading, capitalize the next reference within direction:

```
REVERSE ANGLE - JOHN GLENN

    steps off the elevator in his full space suit.
    Launch workers gather around GLENN.
```

If a character doesn't have any lines, don't capitalize his name. (A rare exception is made for a major character who doesn't speak but nevertheless has a significant, ongoing role in the story.) Typing a character's name in all capitals tells production personnel that the character has lines, which has significant ramifications for casting and budget. Any number of nonspeaking characters can be introduced in a paragraph of direction without anything getting capitalized, until we finally get to a speaking character:

```
    Inside the big top, clowns direct the audience to
    their seats.  A midget walks on tiny stilts.  A lion
    tamer works his big cats in a giant cage.  Seven
    Russian acrobats fly through the air.  A popcorn
    vendor hawks his wares.  Girls covered in gaudy
    sequins ride elephants.  And in the center ring, the
    MASTER OF CEREMONIES calls into his microphone:

                        MASTER OF CEREMONIES
              Ladies and gentlemen, boys and
              girls --
```

• *How to handle the reintroduction of a speaking character who appears at various ages*

Sometimes we meet a character at a given age, say twenty years old, and then meet the same character as a 70-year-old. Does the character's name get capitalized a second time when the 70-year-old version is introduced? The answer depends on whether or not one actor is expected to play both roles. Capitalizing the second introduction implies that a different actor will play the second role. In the movie *A Beautiful Mind*, actor Russell Crowe plays John Nash at many different ages throughout the character's life, from a young student arriving at college to an old man receiving a Nobel Prize. Because the same actor plays the character of John Nash at all of those different ages, Nash would properly be introduced and his name typed in all capitals just one time, when the character of the young student first appears on screen. In the movie *Big Fish*, the main character is played by two actors. Ewan McGregor plays the young man while Albert Finney plays the older man. This character's name would be introduced and capitalized twice, once for each actor. Often it's an easy call. We meet a character at ages seven and thirty-seven. No question. Two different actors. Or we encounter a character at ages twenty-five and forty. Almost certainly the same actor.

For an example of how a character gets re-introduced when played at a second age by a second actor, let's pretend that *A Beautiful Mind* contains a flashback to John Nash's childhood. We'll see his name capitalized when he's introduced as a college student, and then when he's introduced as a child:

```
An awkward young man makes his way among the
brilliant and urbane young mathematicians: JOHN
NASH.  He's smarter than all of them and he's the
only one who knows it.  As he takes in the faces of
the competition --

FLASHBACK - EXT. WEST VIRGINIA SCHOOLHOUSE - DAY (1935)

An awkward little boy steps onto the yard of a
ramshackle mountain schoolhouse.  It's YOUNG NASH,
age 8.  The raw-boned sons of coal miners stare at
this odd boy.
```

YOUNG NASH could just as correctly be called 8-YEAR-OLD NASH, YOUNG JOHN NASH, JOHNNY NASH, or any other name that wouldn't reasonably get confused with Nash in his adult incarnation.

Describing sound effects and offscreen sounds

The second reason for typing words in all capital letters in direction is because they describe a sound effect or an offscreen sound. Three basic rules govern capitalization for sound effects and offscreen sounds:

1.   Type *all sounds* that originate *offscreen* in all capital letters. This includes everything from a ticking clock to a woman's scream to a nuclear explosion, no exceptions.

```
        From somewhere O.S. comes the sound of a
        WOMAN'S SCREAM.

        FOOTSTEPS can be heard in the room overhead.

        The MOAN of a CAT somewhere in the shadows
        keeps Marc awake.
```

```
            Linda whirls toward a KNOCK at her bedroom
            door.

            Behind the curtain, CHILDREN are LAUGHING.
```

2.   **Type all *sound effects* that originate *onscreen* in all capital letters.** A sound effect, for purposes of this rule, is any natural, artificial, or mechanical sound not produced live in front of the camera by an actor. This includes ticking clocks and nuclear explosions but *not* a woman's scream, so long as it originates onscreen in the lungs of a living, breathing actor.

```
            Maverick quick-draws his SIX-SHOOTER and FIRES.

            The laughing, screaming, shouting, giggling
            children knock over the VASE, which SHATTERS on
            the bricks.

            MUSIC PLAYS ON the old transistor RADIO.
```

Because they are sound effects, CAPITALIZE the following:

> Guns firing
> Bombs, grenades and fireworks exploding
> Bullets pinging and ricocheting
> Engines revving, idling, purring, roaring or dying
> Brakes grinding
> Tires squealing
> Horns honking
> Vehicles crashing
> Babies crying, burping or wailing (an effect because babies don't perform on cue)
> Animals growling, birds chirping (see "babies" above)
> Glass breaking or shattering
> Lumber splintering
> Radios, TVs, recorders, boom boxes, CD players and MP3 players playing
> Telephones and doorbells ringing
> Teletypes chattering
> Robots and computers beeping or clicking
> Teapots whistling
> Floors creaking
> Hinges squeaking
> Water dripping, splashing, running, roaring or rushing
> Waves crashing

Lightning cracking and thunder rumbling
Wind gusting, whistling or howling
Incorporeal beings speaking or moaning
Any sound that echoes, reverberates or fades away

Because they are natural sounds made live by actors, DON'T CAPITALIZE the following:

Onscreen characters laughing, talking, shouting, screaming, humming, singing, coughing, sneezing or wheezing.
Onscreen characters clapping their hands, snapping their fingers or tapping their pencils or toes.
Onscreen characters knocking on doors.
Onscreen crowds applauding, roaring, cheering the mayor or booing a dictator.
Onscreen musicians playing instruments.

3.   When capitalizing for sound effects and offscreen sounds, **always capitalize both the thing making the sound and the sound it makes.** For example, if a gun fires, type, "The GUN FIRES," because the gun is the thing making the sound and "fires" is the sound the gun makes. Other examples:

The CHERRY BOMB smokes silently for several long seconds, then abruptly EXPLODES.

Gonzalez picks up the RINGING PHONE.

There's a flash of lightning, followed by the LOW RUMBLE of THUNDER.

The executioner's FOOTSTEPS ECHO off the polished floors.

Chuck turns ON the RADIO. SCRATCHY JAZZ PLAYS. He snaps the RADIO back OFF.

The brawl overturns the JUKE BOX and the MUSIC COMES TO a SCREECHING HALT.

The FIAT SQUEALS around the corner, ENGINE RACING, DOWNSHIFTS and ROARS away up the street, TIRES SCREAMING.

```
A BULLET SHATTERS the WINDOW and PINGS OFF the
seat belt.  The next BULLET RICOCHETS around
the inside of the car.  The third BULLET THUDS
into Markie's chest.

SKYLARKS TWITTER in the morning air.  The BABY
GURGLES happily. The FLOOR CREAKS as Mary
crosses to the WHISTLING TEAPOT.  Her CELL
PHONE RINGS "BROWN-EYED GIRL."  And then all
SOUND FADES SLOWLY to silence.
```

Capitalize the word "sound" only as a last resort, if there is nothing more specific to describe what is heard:

```
The children wake to the sound of a DISTANT
MARCHING BAND.

Somewhere in the bushes, Markie hears a SOFT
SOUND.
```

Describing camera direction

The third and final reason for typing words in all capital letters in direction is because they describe camera direction. A single, three-part rule governs capitalization for camera direction: **Always capitalize 1) the word "camera"; 2) any movement the camera makes; and 3) any prepositions that relate to the camera or its movement.**

1.   Always capitalize the word "camera":

```
The horse gallops directly AT CAMERA.
```

This applies of course only when "camera" refers to the camera filming the movie, not to prop cameras *in* the movie:

```
The photographer swings his still camera round
and round over his head, then lets it fly PAST
CAMERA.
```

If the words "we" or "us" are used in place of the word "camera," do not capitalize them:

```
We PASS ABOVE the battle and SWOOP INTO the
clouds, a flock of doves passing just BELOW us.
```

Never capitalize the phrase "we see":

```
We see a duck floating in the oily water.
```

It's a good idea to avoid using the formulation "we see." Instead of writing, "We see a duck floating in the oily water," write, "A duck floats in the oily water." It's more economical and avoids forcing the reader and writer onto the page in the form of "we."

2.   Capitalize any movement the camera makes (whether the word "camera" is actually used or is only implied):

```
CAMERA TRACKS Foster as he tumbles down the
rocky slope.

As the jury enters, PAN their grim faces.

Winters climbs in the Volvo.  RACK FOCUS TO
Sommers climbing out of the Saab.

Sailors pour onto the deck of the destroyer.
TILT UP to see Japanese Zeroes racing over
their heads.

CAMERA MOVES WITH Englund ACROSS the trading
floor.

As the roar of the unruly crowd builds, ZOOM IN
ON young Charlie, alone in the mob.

Shane stands in the center of Main Street.
CRANE UP until he looks very, very small.

HOLD ON Lamaster's face.

CAMERA FLIES LOW OVER the carnage on Omaha
Beach during the thick of the invasion.
```

3.   Capitalize any prepositions that relate to the camera or its movement. These may relate to the actual movement of the camera or to the movement of someone or something in relation to the camera:

```
CAMERA ROCKETS UP and UP and UP until it FLOATS
ABOVE the smoke of the burning city.
```

```
We FOLLOW Sylvia THROUGH the door, INTO the
crowded disco, UP the long stairway and ALONG a
corridor, PAST a beefy bouncer TOWARD a dying
Muggeridge.
```

```
The balloon floats OVER CAMERA.
```

```
The runner sprints PAST us.
```

```
The biplane flies right AT us.
```

```
Lincoln sits facing the stage, his back TO
CAMERA.
```

```
Adams turns TOWARD CAMERA.
```

• *The expressions "into frame," "out of frame," "into view," and "out of view"*

The words "into frame" and "out of frame" represent camera direction and are always capitalized:

```
Waters steps INTO FRAME.  He lets out a high-pitched
laugh then immediately drops OUT OF FRAME.
```

The words "into view" and "out of view" are sometimes used interchangeably with "into frame" and "out of frame." When they are, they are capitalized:

```
Waters steps INTO VIEW.  He lets out a high-pitched
laugh then immediately drops OUT OF VIEW.
```

At other times, someone or something comes into view not because it has crossed the threshold of the camera's frame (making the words "into view" camera direction), but because it has emerged from behind something else. This is not camera direction and should not be capitalized:

```
Tired of playing hide-and-seek, Waters crawls into
view from his hiding place behind the couch.  Then
he changes his mind and hurries out of view behind
the kitchen door.
```

• *Freeze frame*

The term *freeze frame* refers to an onscreen image that remains still, or frozen, for a period of time. When a moving image freezes midscene, the words "freeze frame" are placed in direction and typed in all capital letters:

```
Golda spots Sam across the tidy fence.  He's in his
best suit.  She's covered with mud from the garden.
His lips curl into a tiny smile.  FREEZE FRAME.
```

If the shot consists of nothing but a still image from start to finish, the words "freeze frame" can appear in the shot heading:

```
FREEZE FRAME - HINDENBURG

At the precise instant flames engulf the airship.
```

A handful of exceptions to prove the rule

A few miscellaneous items that don't fit neatly into the above categories also get typed in all capital letters: *superimpositions*, the words "*ad lib*," certain abbreviations and, optionally, the text of *signs, banners, and headlines*.

• *Superimpositions*

A superimposition occurs when words such as "One Year Later" appear on the screen. The word "superimpose" or just "super" is typed in all capital letters, followed by a colon and the words to be supered in all caps and quotation marks. The words can be set on a line by themselves and centered:

```
SUPERIMPOSE:

          "SOUTH CHINA SEA, 1938"
```

Or they can be embedded within a paragraph of direction:

```
A street car passes.  SUPER: "30 YEARS EARLIER."
```

• *Ad libs*

When actors improvise dialogue, they are said to be speaking "ad lib." The words "ad lib" are always typed in all capital letters:

```
Joanie pops out of the giant cake.  Her grandparents
AD LIB their surprise.
```

- *Capitalized abbreviations*

The abbreviations V.O. and O.S. are always typed in all caps, with periods. O.S. stands for offscreen, or outside the view of the camera. V.O. stands for voice over, which refers to the sound of a voice that originates from some location outside the current scene. In other words, someone standing just outside the frame could be heard speaking O.S. (i.e. from offscreen), while someone speaking by telephone from a location a continent away would only be heard speaking V.O. (i.e. voice over).

- *Signs, banners, and headlines*

The text of a sign, banner, or headline may be typed in all capital letters, at the writer's discretion:

```
The sign at the front of the store reads, "HELP
WANTED."  And below that, in letters not much
smaller, "Japs Need Not Apply."

The kids unfurl a scroll of paper written in bright
crayon.  "HAPPY BIRTHDAY, MISS BEASELY!"

Bobbie pages breathlessly through the paper until
she finds the article headlined: "'MIRACLE' SAVES
GIRL AT BURGER KING."
```

Capitalizing the first letter of direction following a shot heading

The first letter of direction following a shot heading should be capitalized unless the shot heading forms a complete sentence with the direction that follows it. Consider the following examples:

```
CLOSE ON MUSTANG CONVERTIBLE

As its emergency lights flash.

MAGGIE

Grimacing.  She'll never admit it but her shoulder
is killing her.
```

```
EXT. WATER TOWER - NIGHT

Lit up by a ring of floodlights below.
```

But:

```
JOSH

types an urgent command into the keyboard.  The
countdown stops.

CLOSE - CHIHUAHUA

scampers over the counters, lapping up the spilled
beer.
```

What NOT to capitalize: EVERYTHING ELSE

If it doesn't fall into one of the above categories, don't type it in capital letters. Do not capitalize:

Props
Characters' actions
Visual effects
Lighting cues
Character names in direction if it isn't the first time they appear
Nonspeaking character names
The words "we see"
The word "silence"
The abbreviation "b.g." for background
The abbreviation "f.g." for foreground

■ Underscoring in direction

Underscoring, or underlining, may be used in direction for emphasis. Readers of scripts read swiftly and on occasion the judicious use of underscoring can help to ensure that an essential bit of information gets noticed or is given the necessary emphasis. A word of caution, though: Overuse of underscoring in direction looks amateurish and, like the boy who cried wolf, eventually gets ignored.

```
Maggie races up the steps toward the children's
room.  She throws open the door and looks inside.

INT.  CHILDREN'S BEDROOM

All three of the beds are empty.
```

Underscoring of multiple words is always continuous (not <u>All</u> <u>three</u> <u>of</u> <u>the</u> <u>beds</u> <u>are</u> <u>empty</u>). Notice also that the punctuation at the end of the sentence doesn't get underscored.

■ Breaking words with a hyphen in direction

Words in direction may be broken at the right margin of direction with a hyphen:

```
Radcliffe catches the ball in the air.  He's hit,
pirou-ettes on one foot, then falls.
```

Hyphenation is generally infrequent in scripts and should be used sparingly, only to avoid an unacceptably short line. In no case should more than two lines in a row be broken with hyphens.

Dialogue consists of three parts: 1) the name of the character who is speaking; 2) the words that are spoken; and 3) any parenthetical direction related to how the line is spoken or what the character is doing during the speech.

```
                    ¹LOUISE
            ³(rifling her purse)
         ²Where did I put that check?
         Where is it?!
```

■ Character name over dialogue

The first and simplest rule here is that a character's name over dialogue should remain consistent throughout a script. With large numbers of speaking characters in a cast, this isn't always easy to achieve. The name of a character introduced as CAPTAIN MILFORD BROOKS shouldn't appear over dialogue first as CAPTAIN, later as CAPT. BROOKS, and later still as BROOKS. Choose one name for each character and use it consistently over dialogue.

Changing a character's name over dialogue

Sometimes, a character's name over dialogue *must* change. When that happens, it is done in a clear and orderly way. Say a character has been introduced as FEMALE SURGEON and that name appears over her dialogue:

```
A FEMALE SURGEON strides into the operating room.

                    FEMALE SURGEON
         I'm going to need coffee, black,
         stat!  That plate of egg rolls
         from the lounge!  And a breath mint
         for the anesthesiologist!
```

Later, we learn the surgeon's name and decide to switch to using that name over dialogue. We do it like this:

> SURGICAL NURSE
> Good morning, Dr. Crump.

> CRUMP (FEMALE SURGEON)
> 'Morning, sunshine.

Crump picks up a scalpel and goes to work.

> CRUMP
> Keep those breath mints coming.

The first time a character's new name appears over dialogue, the old name appears beside it in parentheses. From then on, the new name is used alone over dialogue. The change has been made in a way that confuses no one.

Numbered names over dialogue

A group of minor characters, say guards or doctors, may be introduced and have only a small number of lines. These characters sometimes never receive individual names like Sal or Throckmorton. They're simply Guard One, Guard Two, and Guard Three. Or First Doctor, Second Doctor, and Third Doctor. Or Assassin #1, Assassin #2, and Assassin #3. Any of these numbering schemes is acceptable. Simply be consistent:

> ASSASSIN #1
> Where are the bullets?

> ASSASSIN #2
> I thought you had the bullets!

> ASSASSIN #3
> We have no <u>bullets</u>?!

Group names over dialogue

Sometimes a group of characters speak together, all saying the same thing, and a plural or group name over dialogue is used:

The MARINES respond in unison.

> MARINES
> Semper fi!

It is also possible to use a plural name over dialogue for a group of characters who speak simultaneous but distinct lines:

```
REPORTERS swarm around the mayor.

                    REPORTERS
        Mr. Mayor!/How do you respond to
        the charges?/Will you have to
        drop out of the campaign?/Do you
        deny the allegations?
```

This is the simplest way to handle short bursts of simultaneous dialogue. A more involved method is described later, under the heading *Double, triple or quadruple dialogue.*

Capitalizing McDonald's and DeVries over dialogue

Just like with shot headings, when names like McDonald's and DeVries appear over dialogue, capitalize like this:

```
                    McDONALD'S MANAGER
        C'mon, c'mon.  Who's on registers?

                    DeVRIES
        Ciao now, brown cow.
```


V.O. and O.S.: When we don't see the person talking

Often dialogue is spoken by characters who aren't visible onscreen at the time their voices are heard. When this happens, the abbreviation V.O. or O.S. appears beside the character name over dialogue. Where and when each designation applies has been a source of great confusion among writers. The rule is this: **When a character is physically present in a scene but is simply outside the view of the camera while speaking, he is offscreen and the abbreviation O.S. applies. The abbreviation V.O. applies in every other case:** voices heard over telephones, answering machines, tape recorders, TVs, loudspeakers and radios, the voices of narrators, voices that overlap from preceding or following scenes and voices originating in memory, imagination or hallucination. The abbreviations V.O. and O.S. appear beside the character name, capitalized, with periods, enclosed in parentheses.

Melissa pushes play on her ANSWERING MACHINE. There's a BEEP, then:

> MRS. TEAGUE (V.O.)
> Melissa? Melissa, it's Mom. If you're there, pick up. Sweetheart, it's an emergency. Your daddy cut up all my plastic again.

The sun rises over Walton's Mountain.

> NARRATOR (V.O.)
> That was the last time John Boy ever saw his uncle. But he never forgot the man. Or the lesson he had taught.

A TV behind the bar is PLAYING the NEWS:

> NEWS ANCHOR (V.O.)
> ... Authorities say that the storm is expected to strike about midnight tonight.

Nick snaps up the RINGING PHONE.

> NICK
> This is Nick.

> MARY (V.O.)
> (on phone)
> It's me. I'm still waiting.

Jake tumbles through space, the helmet of his space suit shattered, his face a mask of terror, as the space ship drifts away from him.

> MOM (V.O.)
> Jake. Wake up, Jake. You're going to miss the school bus.

```
INT. JAKE'S BEDROOM - MORNING

His eyes snap open and he looks up at his
longsuffering Mom.  Gives her a queasy smile.
```

All of the above examples are designated V.O. because the voice comes from somewhere outside the physical location of the scene. In the next example, the voice originates nearby, but outside the view of the camera, and is therefore designated O.S.:

```
Queeg turns at the sound of Ned calling from outside
the locked door.

                         NED (O.S.)
          I'll break down this door, you
          don't open it.  Don't think I
          won't.
```

Using "Voice" instead of V.O. and O.S.

An older, less common but still legitimate method of handling offscreen voices and voice overs is to use the word "voice" beside the unseen speaker's name:

```
                         MARY'S VOICE
               (on phone)
          It's me.  I'm still waiting.

                         NED'S VOICE
          I'll break down this door,
          you don't open it.  Don't think
          that I won't.
```

When this method is used, offscreen voices and voice overs are handled identically. Whichever method you decide to use, use it consistently throughout the script.

■ The words that are spoken

The actual words that characters speak comprise the vital heart of dialogue. Several guidelines apply. First, for the sake of the actors who will say them, **spell out every spoken word**. Instead of "Lt." type "Lieutenant." Instead of "St." type "Street." Or perhaps "Saint":

>   ZUZU
>   Lieutenant Gi lives on Saint
>   Street.

Grammar, accents, and colloquial speech

Characters speak in a manner consistent with who they are. Their grammar isn't always correct. Their sentences aren't always complete. They talk like real people talk. Consequently, incorrect grammar is common and acceptable in dialogue:

>   SNAKE
>   Ain' t nobody gonna stop me.

Nonstandard spellings may be used when they serve to describe a unique way a character pronounces a word:

>   AGENT GUTHRIE
>   I plan to shoot that fat Eye-talian
>   Al Capone.

>   STEVE MARTIN
>   Well excuuuuuuse me.

Accents can be suggested by judiciously modifying the spellings of words.

>   TEX
>   We' re fixin' to do some dumpster
>   divin' .

A strong word of caution here: When this sort of thing is overdone, it's murder to read. An accent can be suggested with word choices as well as spelling changes, and a little goes a very long way.

Emphasizing words in dialogue

To give a word or group of words in dialogue special force or emphasis, underscore them:

>   MICAH
>   Not this one. <u>That</u> one.

```
                    SCHMIDT
         Go ahead.  Call your New York
         lawyer.  We will bury you.
```

As with underlining in direction, underscoring of multiple words is always continuous (not We will bury you). Notice also that the punctuation at the end of the sentence doesn't get underscored.

If you want to give even greater force to a word or group of words in dialogue, combine capitalization with the underscoring:

```
                    SGT. LITTLE
         Fire your weapons!  FIRE!!!
```

Don't use bold or italics. This rule dates to the era when scripts were typed on Underwoods and boldface and italic type weren't practical. It continues to make sense today because when an original print of a script is photocopied, as it will be if it's widely read, bold and italics can come to look more and more like regular type and the intended emphasis is lost.

Initials and acronyms in dialogue

Initials and acronyms occurring in dialogue should be typed in all capital letters. Initials are typed with periods to indicate to the actor that the letters are to be pronounced individually:

```
                    SCHRECKER
         We met at an I.E.P. for
         L.A.U.S.D.
```

Acronyms are typed without periods to indicate that they are to be pronounced as words:

```
                    SMYTHE
         He left FEMA to run an AIDS
         clinic.
```

This can be an extremely helpful pronunciation aid when the terms are technical and relatively unfamiliar:

```
                    DR. BECKETT
         Push the V-ZIG I.M. before the
         G.C.S.F., which is given sub-Q.
```

The above guidelines notwithstanding, some initials (e.g. TV and FBI) are so familiar that they present no risk of confusion even without periods and no harm is done if the periods are omitted.

Breaking words with a hyphen in dialogue

Unless the word is already hyphenated (e.g. sister-in-law), don't break words at the right margin of dialogue with a hyphen. Instead, move the entire word to the next line and keep it intact. Your actors will thank you. (A necessary exception occurs when a word is so long it can't possibly fit within the margins of dialogue. Sadly, very few such words actually exist.)

■ Parenthetical character direction

Parenthetical character direction refers to words of direction contained in parentheses within a line of dialogue:

```
                    JONAH
              (absolutely terrified)
          Why shouldn't you throw me
          overboard?
                  (eyeing the angry
                   water)
          I can't swim.  And I've a fear
          of fish.


                    SHIPMATE
          And we've a fear of drowning.
                  (looks at his fellow
                   sailors; smiles)
          And there's more of us than
          there are of you.
```

Five rules of parenthetical character direction

Five principal rules govern parenthetical character direction:

1.   Include in parenthetical direction only a description of how a line is spoken or what the character is doing while the line is being spoken. Never include direction for anyone other than the character actually

speaking. Never include technical direction such as sound effects or
camera direction. All of the following are INCORRECT:

<pre>
                        ALYSE
              (Mike enters)
          Hey, what's up?
              (Mike ignores her)
          <u>Hell-o</u>. Earth to Mike.

                        TREVOR
              (PHONE RINGS)
          Trevor Trotter speaking.

                        GRIFFIN
          Stay right there.
              (steps OUT OF FRAME,
               returns)
          I got you this book.
</pre>

All of what appears in parentheses above should be pulled out and
placed in regular direction:

<pre>
    Mike enters.

                        ALYSE
          Hey, what's up?

    Mike ignores her.

                        ALYSE
          <u>Hell-o</u>. Earth to Mike.

    The PHONE RINGS.

                        TREVOR
          Trevor Trotter speaking.

                        GRIFFIN
          Stay right there.

    He steps OUT OF FRAME, returns.

                        GRIFFIN
          I got you this book.
</pre>

2.   **Never capitalize the first letter of parenthetical direction or add a period at the end.** Punctuation consists primarily of commas and semicolons, never a dash, never an ellipsis, and never a final period.

Instead of this:

```
                    HAMLET
              (Relishing the famous
              line.)
         To be or not to be.
```

Do this, lower-casing the first letter and omitting the final punctuation:

```
                    HAMLET
              (relishing the famous
              line)
         To be or not to be.
```

Instead of this:

```
                    NIXON
              (points to recorder...
              signals Haldeman to keep
              quiet -- smiles)
         I just had the new tape system
         installed.  Have to look out for my
         place in history, you know.
```

Do this, replacing the ellipsis and dash with semicolons:

```
                    NIXON
              (points to recorder;
              signals Haldeman to keep
              quiet; smiles)
         I just had the new tape system
         installed.  Have to look out for my
         place in history, you know.
```

As in the example above, multiple directions can be linked with semicolons:

```
                  SGT. SLICK
         Hey, Jerry!
              (waits a beat; throws
              grenade; ducks)
         Catch this.
```

A colon is also sometimes used:

```
                    CENSUS WORKER
          (re: clipboard)
     Sign here.
```

On rare occasions a question mark or exclamation point is used:

```
                    DEFENDANT
          (gulp!)
     I'd love to have dinner with
     you, Your Honor.


                    SHEILA
          (what, me worry?)
     Bring it on.
```

3.   **Don't start parenthetical direction with "he" or "she."** It's understood.

Instead of this:

```
                    SHERIFF
          (he draws his gun)
     Stop right there.
```

Do this:

```
                    SHERIFF
          (draws his gun)
     Stop right there.
```

4.   **Don't let parenthetical direction run to more than four lines.**

Instead of this:

```
                    ROBBIE
     Let me show you something.
          (opens drawer, pulls
          out three brightly
          colored balls and
          starts to juggle;
          drops one and starts
          again; a little
          embarrassed)
     I'm still learning.
```

Do this:

>   ROBBIE
>   Let me show you something.
>
>   He opens a drawer, pulls out three brightly
>   colored balls and starts to juggle. He drops
>   one and starts again.
>
>   ROBBIE
>   (a little embarrassed)
>   I'm still learning.

5.   **Don't place parenthetical direction at the end of a speech.**

Instead of this:

>   JOJO
>   (laughing)
>   Don't you just wish.
>   (touches his arm)

Do this:

>   JOJO
>   (laughing)
>   Don't you just wish.
>
>   She touches his arm.

Sotto voce, beat, re:

Three terms get heavy use in parenthetical direction: *sotto voce*, *beat* and *re:*.

Sotto voce is Italian for "soft voice" and is used in parenthetical direction to instruct an actor to deliver a line quietly or under his breath:

>   PRESIDENTIAL CANDIDATE
>   I can't tell you how happy I am
>   to be in North Dakota today.
>   (fake smile; sotto voce)
>   Because I'm not.

Sotto voce is sometimes shortened to just "sotto":

```
                    BURGLAR
               (sotto)
          Hand me that crowbar.
```

A beat is a script term meaning a short pause. It appears often in both direction and parenthetical character direction:

```
                    NICHOLS
          Let's walk.
               (beat)
          On second thought, let's ride.
```

Beats come in several flavors:

```
                    SAMPSON
               (short beat)
          Why not?
```

```
                    DELILAH
               (long beat; shakes
                her head)
          We're dead.
```

```
                    RUNNING HORSE
          Know what I think?
               (two full beats;
                grins)
          Hell, I don't even know what I
          think.
```

```
                    Z
               (half a beat too
                slow)
          Of course I love you.
```

The term "re:" appears often in parenthetical direction, meaning "with regard to":

```
                    WHITE
               (re: his haircut)
          What d'ya think?
```

■ Foreign language dialogue and subtitles

When dialogue is in a foreign language, it can be written in the desired language, like this:

                              LARS OLE
                    Hvor er du, Hans?

If you want the foreign dialogue to be subtitled, indicate that in parenthetical direction, in lower case letters, then type the dialogue in English, saving yourself years of foreign language study:

                              LARS OLE
                        (in Norwegian;
                         subtitled)
                    Where are you, Hans?

If an entire conversation is subtitled, that can be indicated in direction, in all caps, preceding the exchange:

        The men speak in German with SUBTITLES:

                              HELMUT
                    Have you ever seen a U-boat?

                              WERNER
                    Never. But isn't that the whole
                    idea?

■ Song lyrics in dialogue

Unless the movie is a musical, type the song lyrics in upper and lower case letters, enclosed in quotation marks. Observe the lyrical line endings by wrapping the ends of long lines and indenting the wrapped text two spaces:

                              TEX
                    "Home, home on the range
                    Where the deer and the antelope play
                    Where seldom is heard a discouraging
                      word
                    And the skies are not cloudy all
                      day."

If the movie *is* a musical, type song lyrics in all capital letters, without quotation marks or ending punctuation:

```
                    TEX
        HOME, HOME ON THE RANGE
        WHERE THE DEER AND THE ANTELOPE PLAY
        WHERE SELDOM IS HEARD A DISCOURAGING
           WORD
        AND THE SKIES ARE NOT CLOUDY ALL
           DAY
```

■ Breaking a page in the middle of dialogue

Never break a page in the middle of a sentence in dialogue. Always split the page between sentences, add (MORE) at the bottom of the page, and (CONT'D) beside the character name at the top of the following page:

```
                    FRANCONI
        The treatment lasts just over
        a year.
                    (MORE)
    -----page break -----
                    FRANCONI (CONT'D)
        It starts with fractionated
        radiotherapy combined with a
        chemotherapeutic agent.
```

Not:

```
                    FRANCONI
        The treatment lasts just over
        a year.  It starts with
                    (MORE)
    -----page break -----
                    FRANCONI (CONT'D)
        fractionated radiotherapy
        combined with a chemotherapeutic
        agent.
```

Never break dialogue with parenthetical direction at the bottom of the page. Instead, carry the parenthetical direction to the top of the following page, like this:

```
                              FRANCONI
                 Vincristine.  It's given outpatient.
                 Intravenously.
                              (MORE)
          -----page break -----
                              FRANCONI (CONT'D)
                      (writing it down)
                 Vincristine.  Look up the side
                 effects.
```

Not:

```
                              FRANCONI
                 Vincristine.  It's given outpatient.
                 Intravenously.
                      (writing it down)
                              (MORE)
          -----page break -----
                              FRANCONI (CONT'D)
                 Vincristine.  Look up the side
                 effects.
```

■ Adding (cont'd), (CONT'D) or (continuing) when a speech is broken by direction

In years past, it was customary when a character's speech resumed after being broken by direction to indicate that it was a continuing speech. This was accomplished by adding (cont'd) or (CONT'D) beside the character name or the word "continuing" in parenthetical direction beneath the character name. It was done like this:

```
                              JONESY
                 Come in.  Sit down.

          The PHONE RINGS.

                              JONESY (CONT'D)
                 I'll get that.
```

Or:

```
                              JONESY
                 Come in.  Sit down.
```

```
The PHONE RINGS.

                             JONESY (cont'd)
                 I'll get that.
```

Or:

```
                             JONESY
                 Come in.  Sit down.

The PHONE RINGS.

                             JONESY
                        (continuing)
                 Come in.  Sit down.
```

In each case, the determining factor was that the same character was continuing to speak, direction notwithstanding, without an intervening speech by another character.

But here's the thing. **Marking continuing speeches is no longer standard practice in Hollywood and hasn't been for at least 20 years.** Writers now regularly dispense with indicating that a speech is continuing, saving words and streamlining their scripts in the process. If your script software is set to add (cont'd) or (CONT'D) or (continuing) when a speech is broken by direction, feel free to turn it off. (**An important caveat:** The one place this practice remains standard is half-hour television formats. See *multi-camera film format*.)

■ Double, triple, and quadruple dialogue

As a more flexible alternative to group dialogue, as described earlier, when multiple characters speak at the same time their dialogue can be typed in side-by-side columns like this:

```
          SLADKEY                          BROWN
I told him but he didn't        I told you exactly what
listen.  He never               to say.  I told you
listens.                        what to do if he didn't
     (not listening)            listen.  Why don't you
What do you want me to          ever listen?
do?
```

Complete, separate conversations can run in parallel columns:

SLADKEY Is Manny there?	LISZT I'm calling from Doctor Brockman's office.
MARIA (V.O.) He's at the mill.	JUNE (V.O.) Are my results back?
SLADKEY Really? I thought he was working nights now.	LISZT Not yet. There was a mix-up at the lab. We need you to come back for another blood draw.
MARIA (V.O.) He's filling in for someone out sick.	
SLADKEY Tell him I called.	JUNE (V.O.) Ah no. You're kidding me.

Two, three, four and even five characters can speak simultaneously:

                    SLADKEY
               Kids, I'm home. Who wants
               pizza?

RACHEL	HOPE	PETER
Where's it from?	I want sausage.	I'm not hungry.

Sladkey opens in the box on the counter.

                    SLADKEY
               Just get in here. I got
               pepperoni.

RACHEL	HOPE	PETER	EMILY
From <u>where</u>?	Not sausage?	I'm not hungry!	Yeah!!!

                    SLADKEY
               Where's Pam?

Pam enters from the bathroom.

PAM	RACHEL	HOPE	PETER	EMILY
Here I am!	Pam who?	Pam hates pizza.	Pam owes me five dollars!	Yeah, Pam!!!

Bear in mind that simultaneous dialogue can be tedious to read and should be used sparingly.

Margins for simultaneous dialogue

Margins for simultaneous dialogue are as follows:

• *Two simultaneous speakers*

1.   Dialogue
                First speaker
                        Left margin is 1.9" (position 19)
                        Right margin is 4.5" (position 40)
                Second speaker
                        Left margin is 4.0" (position 45)
                        Right margin is 2.0" (position 65)

2.   Character name over dialogue
                First speaker
                        Left margin is 2.7" (position 27)
                Second speaker
                        Left margin is 5.2" (position 52)

• *Three simultaneous speakers*

1.   Dialogue
                First speaker
                        Left margin is 1.7" (position 17)
                        Right margin is 5.3" (position 32)
                Second speaker
                        Left margin is 3.5" (position 35)
                        Right margin is 3.5" (position 50)
                Third speaker
                        Left margin is 5.3" (position 53)
                        Right margin is 1.7" (position 68)

2.   Character name over dialogue
                First speaker
                        Left margin is 2.2" (position 22)
                Second speaker
                        Left margin is 4.0" (position 40)
                Third speaker
                        Left margin is 5.8" (position 58)

• *Four simultaneous speakers*

1.   Dialogue

First speaker
Left margin is 1.6" (position 16)
Right margin is 5.8" (position 27)
Second speaker
Left margin is 3.0" (position 30)
Right margin is 4.4" (position 41)
Third speaker
Left margin is 4.4" (position 44)
Right margin is 3.0" (position
Fourth speaker
Left margin is 5.8" (position 58)
Right margin is 1.6" (position 69)

2.   Character name over dialogue

First speaker
Left margin is 1.9" (position 19)
Second speaker
Left margin is 3.3" (position 33)
Third speaker
Left margin is 4.7" (position 47)
Fourth speaker
Left margin is 6.1" (position 61)

TRANSITIONS

Transitions are the various methods one shot or scene changes to the next. They include *cuts*, *dissolves*, *fades*, and *wipes*:

```
FADE IN:

THREE GIANT PUMPKINS

baking under a Texas sun.

                                    DISSOLVE TO:

LITTLE BOY

Striking a match.

                                    CUT TO:

SCARECROW

Burning brightly.   The boy watches.

                                    WIPE TO:

300-POUND FARMER

has the boy by the ear, dragging him toward the
woodshed.

                                    FADE OUT.
```

With the exception of FADE IN, all transitions are typed 6.0" from the left edge of the page.

■ Fades

A *fade in* is a gradual transition from a solid color, usually black, to a filmed image. A *fade out* is the reverse, a gradual transition from a filmed image to black. FADE IN: is typed at the left margin for direction in all capital letters, followed by a colon:

```
FADE IN:
```

FADE OUT. is typed 6.0" from the left edge of the page in all capital letters followed by a period:

```
                                        FADE OUT.
```

Feature film scripts usually begin with a FADE IN: and end with a FADE OUT., but they don't necessarily have to.

Television scripts are usually divided by several act breaks representing commercial breaks, and each act typically begins with a FADE IN: and ends with a FADE OUT.

FADE TO BLACK can be used as an alternative to FADE OUT:

```
                                     FADE TO BLACK.
```

When a transition consists of a fade from a filmed image to a white screen write, "FADE TO WHITE":

```
                                     FADE TO WHITE.
```

■ Cuts

The cut, an instantaneous shift from one shot to the next, is the most common transition:

```
                                           CUT TO:
```

When no transition is indicated, a cut is assumed. An entire script can actually be written without any transitions being indicated at all and the reader will assume that every transition is a cut.

Why then would a writer ever specify a cut?

Some writers use "CUT TO" to establish a sense of rhythm or pace by placing a CUT TO: after every shot in an action sequence. A CUT TO: also creates white space on a page that might otherwise look too dense. And a CUT TO: added at the end of a sequence can give a heightened sense of finality, a more distinct sense that one thing has ended and a new thing has begun.

Note that CUT TO: is typed in all capital letters and followed by a colon. Cuts come in various flavors, including the *hard cut*, which describes a transition that is jarring:

```
Jenny smells the rose.

                                 HARD CUT TO:


SCREAMING LOCOMOTIVE

bearing down on her.
```

The *quick cut* is not one that happens faster than any other, but one that happens *sooner* than it otherwise might:

```
And just as Jason turns toward the blinding light --

                                 QUICK CUT TO:
```

A *time cut* emphasizes that time is passing from one shot to the next:

```
Far above the surf, Sweeney dozes on dry sand.

                                 TIME CUT TO:


SAME SCENE - TWO HOURS LATER

A wave washes over Sweeney and wakes him,
sputtering.  The tide has come in.
```

A *match cut* specifies a cut in which the image in the first shot either visually or thematically matches the image in the following shot:

```
The fat lady opens her mouth to sing.

                                 MATCH CUT TO:


LITTLE SALLY SALTER

Screaming like a banshee.
```

A *cut to black* (or white or any other color) can be used in lieu of a fade to black for dramatic effect, and is followed by a period:

> Dr. Drake positions the bone saw over Jimmy's leg.
>
>   CUT TO BLACK.

■ Dissolves

A dissolve is a gradual transition from one image to another. It often implies a passage of time:

> Sister Margaret sits down outside the courtroom to wait.
>
>   DISSOLVE TO:
>
> INT. COURTHOUSE - LATER
>
> Hours have passed and Sister Margaret is still here, still waiting.

Like cuts, dissolves come in a variety of flavors. There are slow dissolves, fast dissolves, and the wavy effect known as a ripple dissolve, often used to suggest a transition into daydream or imagination:

> Slim sits in his wheelchair and stares at the horse.
>
>   RIPPLE DISSOLVE TO:
> HEAVENLY PASTURE
>
> Slim rides at a full gallop, like the cowboy he once was.

If the transition is so long that it extends beyond the right margin and wraps to a second line, back it up so that it all fits on one line:

> Josh and Heather stand hand in hand on the beach, staring out to sea.
>
>   UNBELIEVABLY SLOW DISSOLVE TO:
>
> SUNSET OVER PACIFIC

■ Wipes

A wipe is a stylized transition in which the new image slides, or wipes, over the top of the old one:

```
BATMAN AND ROBIN

leap into the Batmobile.  TIRES SPIN, flame spews -

                                        WIPE TO:

EXT. GOTHAM CITY POLICE HQ - DAY

The BATMOBILE SKIDS to a stop and the dynamic duo
dismounts.
```

■ Breaking a page at a transition

When breaking a page at a transition, always break *after* the transition, not before. If the transition must be moved to the following page, some part of the preceding scene must go with it. With the exception of FADE IN, **a page must never begin with a transition.**

PUNCTUATION

The subject of punctuation in scripts merits special attention.

■ Period

A *period* at the end of a sentence is always followed by two spaces. However, a period that is part of the abbreviation EXT. or INT. in a shot heading is followed by just one space:

```
EXT. DESTROYER
```

■ Ellipsis

An *ellipsis* is three periods followed by a single space. It is most commonly used in dialogue to indicate that a character's speech has trailed off, many times before starting again:

```
                    MARVIN
          I'd like to say I'll help you but
          I just... I don't know.
```

An ellipsis is also used when we join a character midspeech:

```
                    NEWS ANCHOR (V.O.)
          ... Severe weather moving toward
          Wyandotte County with strong winds.
```

Ellipses are sometimes grossly overused. If a comma will suffice, use a comma. Reserve the ellipsis for its specialized uses.

■ Dash

A *dash* is two hyphens in sequence, with a space before and a space after. It is used in both dialogue and direction to set off parenthetical material:

```
          He's wearing a floppy hat -- the kind worn by
          Norwegian fishermen -- and staggering around like a
          serious drunk.
```

It is also used when dialogue abruptly breaks off:

```
                              HELGE
                    What the --
```

Never leave a dash dangling on a line by itself:

```
                              PATSY
                    Why anyone would say that is beyond
                    --
```

Instead, carry the last word onto the line with the dash:

```
                              PATSY
                    Why anyone would say that is
                    beyond --
```

■ Hyphen

In scripts, the *hyphen* is used in the ordinary way, to hyphenate words like mother-in-law and three-year-old, and to break longer words at the ends of lines of direction:

```
          Teddy races toward the tracks, trying to beat the loco-
          motive to the crossing.
```

Use moderation when hyphenating at the ends of lines of *direction*, and never hyphenate the ends of more than two lines in a row.

Don't hyphenate words at the ends of lines of *dialogue* (unless they're already hyphenated, like writer-director). Instead of this:

```
                              DR. MATHIS
                    Based on the imaging today, medullo-
                    blastoma is a possibility.
```

Do this:

```
                              DR. MATHIS
                    Based on the imaging today,
                    medulloblastoma is a possibility.
```

The hyphen gets special treatment in shot headings. When used to separate elements in shot headings, the hyphen is sandwiched between two spaces, one before and one after:

```
CLOSE SHOT - CLAW HAMMER
```

Hyphenate compound words when they are used like this:

```
The horse is a two-year-old.  She's a two-year-old
horse.
```

But not when they are used like this:

```
The horse is two years old.
```

■ Quotation marks

Quotation marks are placed around all quoted material, plus titles of:

> songs
> poems
> short stories
> television series
> newspaper articles
> magazine articles

Periods and commas always go *inside* the quotation marks:

```
On the monitors, reruns are playing of "Gilligan's
Island," "The Beverly Hillbillies" and "Leave it to
Beaver."
```

Semicolons and colons always go *outside* quotation marks:

```
Simon hums "Clementine"; Trevino pens the names of
what he calls "my boys": Johnny Walker and Jack
Daniels.
```

Question marks and exclamation points go *inside* quotation marks when they are part of the original quotation:

```
The banner at the front of the church reads,
"Hallelujah!"
```

```
     Griffin laughs too loud at the "Got Milk?"
     commercial.
```

Question marks and exclamation points go *outside* when they are *not* part of the original quotation:

```
     The horse leaps through the flames while the rider
     whistles "The William Tell Overture"!
```

```
     Who could have guessed he'd need to know the words
     of Frost's "The Road Not Taken"?
```

■ Underscoring

Underscoring of multiple words is always continuous and the punctuation at the end of the sentence is not underscored. It should look like this:

```
     The money is gone.
```

Not this:

```
     The money is gone.
```

And not this:

```
     The money is gone.
```

Underscore:

> Names of ships
> Names of spacecraft
> Names of planes
> Book titles
> Magazine titles
> Newspaper titles
> Movie titles
> Play titles

```
          Spread on the desk are a copy of the Times,
          Milton's Paradise Lost, and Hamlet, plus books
          about the bomber Enola Gay and the destroyer
          Madison.
```

■ Punctuation and capitalization in direct address

Direct address refers to occasions in dialogue when a character uses the name of the person he is directly speaking to, or addressing. **Always set a name used in direct address apart with commas:**

> SAL
> Hi, Deb. How's it going, Marge?
> Nikki, you mind passing the peas?

Plus, just as you would capitalize the first letter of a proper name, capitalize the first letter of any name used *in place of* a proper name in direct address:

> WILLIAM
> (greeting his guests)
> Hello, Dad. Hi, Mom. How are you,
> Coach? Nice to see you, Sarge.
> You too, Officer. And, Your Honor,
> wow, what an honor!

But don't capitalize *pet names*, *terms of endearment* and the like:

> WILLIAM
> It was a great party, honey.   I
> mean it, sweetheart.
> (to tipsy guest)
> Time to head home, pal.

And don't capitalize improper names (e.g. mom, coach, sergeant) when they aren't being used in direct address:

> WILLIAM
> What a party! My dad was there.
> So was my mom and my high school
> track coach and my old drill
> sergeant and Judge Lemon and
> that nice police officer who
> looks like Carl Malden.

THE EVOLUTION OF A SCRIPT FROM FIRST DRAFT TO PRODUCTION DRAFT

The first draft of a script can look different from a production draft in two important ways: the absence or presence of scene numbers and the absence or presence of CONTINUEDs at the tops and bottoms of pages.

■ CONTINUEDs at the tops and bottoms of pages

When a scene continues from one page to the next, a production draft includes the word (CONTINUED) at the bottom of the first page and the word CONTINUED: at the top of the second page.

> (CONTINUED) is double-spaced down from the last line of text and begins 6.0" from the left paper edge. It is typed in all capital letters, inside parentheses.

> CONTINUED: is double-spaced down from the page number and begins 1.7" from the left paper edge. It is typed in all capital letters and is followed by a colon.

A page broken with CONTINUEDs looks like this:

```
EXT. BATTLEFIELD - DAWN

The sun rises crimson over the fallen soldiers.  Ragged
children move among the dead, searching for survivors.
Or a serviceable pair of boots.

                                          (CONTINUED)
```

```
CONTINUED:

                        UNION CAPTAIN
               You younguns, git!
                         (turning to his
                          men)
               Ever' body knows his job.  Let's
               git to it!

     The men start reluctantly across the field.

                                          CUT TO:
```

Only use CONTINUEDs when a scene is broken between pages. When a scene ends at the bottom of a page and a new scene begins at the top of the following page, don't add CONTINUEDs:

```
     INT. CLOSET - DAY

     Schmidt listens as the FOOTSTEPS RECEDE.  He turns the
     handle and pushes open the closet door.
```

```
     INT. HALLWAY - DAY

     Schmidt pokes his head into the hall and looks both ways.
     Sees the coast is clear.  He steps into the hall.
```

A script may use CONTINUEDs at any stage, but standard format *requires* that they be used when scene numbers are added.

Adding CONTINUEDs at the tops and bottoms of pages takes away space that would otherwise be filled by script content. Consequently, the page count increases when CONTINUEDs are added, usually by about 11%.

■ Scene numbers

Only a script that has reached preproduction should have *scene numbers*. Prior to preproduction, a script should not have scene numbers.

When scene numbers are added to a script, scenes are numbered consecutively beginning at 1, and every shot heading receives a number. (An alternative but less common method numbers only the master scene headings, those that move the action to a new location or a new period of time.)

Scene numbers are typed on both the left and right sides of the shot heading, like this:

```
22        EXT. GRANT'S HEADQUARTERS - NIGHT                        22
```

The left scene number begins 1.0" from the left paper edge.

The right scene number begins 7.4" from the left paper edge.

If a shot heading wraps onto a second line, the scene numbers remain on the first line:

```
9         EXT. NEW YORK CITY - CENTRAL PARK - WIDE ANGLE - BALL   9
          FIELD - DAY
```

When a scene continues from one page to the next, the scene numbers are placed on the same line as the CONTINUED:

```
121       EXT. BATTLEFIELD - DAWN                                121

          The sun rises crimson over the fallen soldiers.  Ragged
          children move among the dead, searching for survivors.
          Or a serviceable pair of boots.

                                            (CONTINUED)
```

```
                                                           109.


121       CONTINUED:                                             121

                              UNION CAPTAIN
                        You younguns, git!
```

If the above scene which begins on page 108 and continues on page 109 is long enough to extend onto page 110, a (2) is placed inside parentheses beside the CONTINUED on page 110:

121   CONTINUED: (2)   121

> SERGEANT
> Gather those guns right here.

Don't be confused. Even though page 110 is the third page of the scene, it is the second CONTINUED page of the scene, and therefore gets a (2).

If the scene kept going, page 111 would get a CONTINUED: (3) and page 112 would get a CONTINUED: (4), and so on until there is a new scene with a new scene number.

When scene numbers are locked

As a script moves through preproduction it is eventually *boarded*, that is a production board is made up based on the scene numbers. Before a script is boarded, it is proper to renumber the scenes when changes are made that add or omit scenes. But after a script is boarded, the scene numbers are locked and shouldn't be changed. Production personnel are working based on the scene numbers that existed at the time the script was boarded.

Omitted scenes

If a scene in a locked script is omitted, it should be indicated as follows:

121   OMITTED   121

122   INT. GRANT'S TENT - NIGHT   122

     Officers have gathered to await word from the general.

In that way, all scene numbers are accounted for and there is no uncertainty about what became of scene 121.

If two scenes are omitted, indicate the omission like this:

```
120     OMITTED                                               120
&                                                             &
121                                                           121


122     INT. GRANT'S TENT - NIGHT                             122

        Officers have gathered to await word from the general.
```

If a group of more than two scenes is omitted, indicate the omission as follows:

```
118     OMITTED                                               118
thru                                                          thru
121                                                           121


122     INT. GRANT'S TENT - NIGHT                             122

        Officers have gathered to await word from the general.
```

Numbering "A" scenes

If a new scene is added in a locked script, it is given a new, unique number, in this case 121A:

```
121     OMITTED                                               121


121A    EXT. NIGHT SKY                                        121A

        Clouds cover the full moon.

122     INT. GRANT'S TENT - NIGHT                             122

        Officers have gathered to await word from Grant.
```

If two or more scenes had been added, they would be numbered 121A, 121B, 121C, and so on. In rare instances more than 26 scenes are inserted and the whole alphabet is expended. When that happens, scene 121Z is followed by 121AA, 121BB, 121CC, and so on.

Add a hyphen to scenes lettered with an I or an O so that the letters aren't confused with numbers:

```
121-I   OMITTED                                          121-I
thru                                                     thru
121-O                                                    121-O
```

If a new scene is added at some later date between scenes 121 and 121A, it is numbered A121A:

```
121     OMITTED                                          121


A121A   ANGLE ON CAMPFIRE                                A121A

        Sparks fly up.


121A    EXT. NIGHT SKY                                   121A

        Clouds cover the full moon.


122     INT. GRANT'S TENT - NIGHT                        122

        Officers have gathered to await word from the general.
```

If two or more scenes had been added, they would be numbered A121A, B121A, C121A, and so on.

The principal is that scene A1 precedes scene 1 and scene 1A follows scene 1.

■ Colored paper

The first time a script receives wide distribution to production personnel, the pages are white. Subsequent versions of the script are distributed on colored paper to avoid the confusion of people working from different versions of the same script. The director can say, "Do you have the buff draft?" and the star can answer, "Buff? I'm still working from the green draft."

In the United States, the standard progression of colors is:

> white
> blue
> pink
> yellow
> green

goldenrod
buff
salmon
cherry
tan

After tan the cycle repeats, starting over with white. Overseas productions often include other paper colors.

■ Revision marks

Once a script has received wide distribution, subsequent versions of the script should contain *revision marks* to help production personnel quickly locate the changes. The revision marks go in the right margin beside each line that contains changes, 7.8" from the left edge of the page. The most common revision mark is the *asterisk*:

```
121    OMITTED                                           121


121A   ANGLE ON CAMPFIRE                                 121A  *

       Sparks fly up.                                          *


121B   EXT. NIGHT SKY                                    121B  *

       Clouds cover the full moon.                             *


122    INT. GRANT'S TENT - NIGHT                         122

          Officers have gathered to await word from the general.
```

If there are so many changes on a given page that more than ten asterisks would be required, a single asterisk goes at the top of the page, to the right of the page number:

<pre>
                                                   110.   *

121   CONTINUED: (2)   121

                         SERGEANT
                 Gather those guns right here.
</pre>

■ Full drafts vs. revised pages

Many times, after a script has already received wide distribution to production personnel, extensive changes are made involving more than half the pages in the script and a whole new, full draft is issued. When this happens, the script is *repaginated.* That is, pages are renumbered with text moving up to fill in the space where omissions are made, and text moving down to make room for added material.

At other times, only a few pages are changed and only those *revised pages* (also called simply *revisions*) are issued. In this case, if a page has no changes, it isn't reprinted. Production personnel replace just the changed pages in their existing scripts. Not only does this practice save paper and expense, it preserves much of the current script and all of the many handwritten notes that frequently cover the pages of a script in preproduction or production.

Say there's a change on page 7 of a full draft of a script that was distributed on blue paper. The change is typed **with revisions marks indicating the location of changes**, the new page 7 is printed on the next color of paper, pink, and distributed. Recipients pull the old blue page 7 out of their scripts and put the new pink page 7 in its place.

In practice, of course, a set of revisions may involve forty or fifty or even sixty revised pages. The principle, though, remains the same. The old pages are pulled out and the new pages are put in their place. The process of issuing revised pages frequently continues until the script contains every possible color of paper and is accurately described as a *rainbow script.*

Revision slugs

Every page of a set of revised pages bears a *revision slug* at the top of the page, on the same line as the page number, that includes the title (in all capital letters) and date of the revisions:

```
UNDER THE TABLE - Rev. 3/11/04                    17.
```

For series television, include both the series title (all caps) and episode title (upper and lower case with quotation marks), plus the revision date:

```
ALIAS - "A Life Apart" - Rev. 2/21/04            59.
```

The revision slug begins 1.7" from the left edge of the page.

Deleting material from revised pages

If material is deleted from a page, that page remains short. In the following example, scene 23 is being omitted from page 12 of a script titled *Grant* in a set of revisions dated 1/1/04:

```
GRANT - Rev. 1/1/04 12.

22 EXT. TENT - NIGHT       22

   The men gather their
   weapons.

23 OMITTED                23 *
```

```
                          13.

24 EXT. NIGHT SKY         24

   The moon is bright.

25 INT. GRANT'S TENT      25

   Soldiers enter and
   exit.  The general
   isn't here at the
   moment.  It's clear
   there's a great deal
   of tension in the air.
   CANNON FIRE can be
   heard IN the DISTANCE.

   Grant suddenly strides
   into the tent, jerks
   off his gloves and
   unrolls a map.  His
   face is covered with
   grime.
```

Material from the following pages can't be allowed to flow onto the revised page to fill the empty space, because if those pages have no changes, they aren't going to be reprinted. They must remain unchanged. This forces page 12 to remain a short page. It then fits correctly into the existing script.

"A" pages

But what do you do if enough new material is added to a page that it forces the subsequent text off the bottom of the page? Let's say that a couple of days have passed since the set of revisions described above. Today, a quarter-page scene needs to be added to page 13, but page 14 has no changes. The extra material from page 13 can't be allowed to flow onto page 14, because page 14 isn't going to be reprinted. Instead, page 13A is created to hold the overflow text and is printed along with the rest of the revised pages. Production personnel will pull the old page 13 out of their scripts and insert the new pages 13 and 13A in its place. The old page 14 will remain in the script unchanged and the new pages will fit correctly into the existing script:

```
    GRANT - Rev. 1/3/04 13.

24  EXT. NIGHT SKY          24

    The moon is bright.

24A EXT. RIVER - NIGHT      24A*

    Confederate snipes        *
    wade silently across,     *
    their long, deadly        *
    rifles held high.         *

25  INT. GRANT'S TENT       25

    Soldiers enter and
    exit.  The general
    isn't here at the
    moment.  It's clear
    there's a great deal
    of tension in the air.

            (CONTINUED)
```

```
    GRANT - Rev. 1/3/04 13.

25  CONTINUED:              25

    CANNON FIRE can be
    heard IN the DISTANCE.

    Grant suddenly strides
    into the tent, jerks
    off his gloves and
    unrolls a map.  His
    face is covered with
    grime.
```

If needed, a "B" page can follow an "A" page, followed by a "C" page, and so on.

Runs of revised pages

When two or more pages in a row contain changes, they constitute a *run of revised pages*. Runs of pages receive special treatment. Since every page in the run has changes and is going to be reprinted, material can flow from page to page within the run. Say there are changes on pages 90, 91, and 92, but page 93 has no changes. A scene is deleted from page 90, making room for material from page 91 to flow forward onto page 90 and fill the empty space. Material from page 92 then flows forward onto page 91. Page 92, the last page in the run, becomes the short page. Page 93 remains undisturbed and the new pages fit correctly into the existing script:

```
GRANT - Rev. 1/7/04 90.

51   EXT. WHITE HOUSE        51

     A military carriage
     rolls to a stop.
     General Grant and an
     aide step out.


52   OMITTED                 52 *


53   INT. WHITE HOUSE        53
     CORRIDOR

     Grant and his aide are
     escorted inside.  The
     general is recognized.
     People stop to watch
     him pass.
```

```
GRANT - Rev. 1/7/04 91.

54   INT. LINCOLN'S PRIVATE 54
     QUARTERS

     Grant and Lincoln
     confer in grave, soft
     voices.  Their words
     can't be made out.  The
     aide stands at a          *
     respectful distance.      *

     Finally Lincoln
     straightens and shakes
     the general's hand.


55   INT. WHITE HOUSE        55
     CORRIDOR

     Grant and his aide pass
     back out the way they     *
     came in.
```

```
GRANT - Rev. 1/7/04 92.

56   EXT. VIRGINIA COUNTRY- 56
     SIDE - NIGHT

     Grant's special TRAIN
     CHUGS past in thick
     darkness, heading        *
     south.                   *
```

```
                          93.

57   EXT. DIRT ROAD - DAWN 57

     Grant rides astride a
     big gelding.  His
     aide trails him.
     They're riding fast,
     pushing their horses
     hard.


58   EXT. GRANT'S HEAD-      58
     QUARTERS - MORNING

     A hot sun is already
     shining.  A stir rises
     in the camp as Grant
     and his aide arrive.
     Grant dismounts and
     strides into his tent
     without a word to
     anyone.
```

Conversely, say that a scene is *added* to page 90. The extra material can flow onto pages 91 and 92 so long as they also have changes, and if an "A" page must be created it will come at the end of the run:

```
        GRANT - Rev. 1/7/04 90.

51   EXT. WHITE HOUSE        51

     A military carriage
     rolls to a stop.
     General Grant and an
     aide step out.


51A  WHITE HOUSE GUARDS    51A*

     Army troops guarding      *
     the executive residence   *
     stand at attention.       *


52   ON GRANT               52

     He pauses to take in
     the great house that
     will one day be his.

              (CONTINUED)
```

```
        GRANT - Rev. 1/7/04 91.

52   CONTINUED:             52

     His eyes travel up to
     a window in the
     private quarters. He
     sees the tall, stooped    *
     figure of the Pres-
     ident looking back at
     him.


53   INT. WHITE HOUSE       53
     CORRIDOR

     Grant and his aide are
     escorted inside. The
     general is recognized.
     People stop to watch
     him pass.
```

```
        GRANT - Rev. 1/7/04 92.

54   INT. LINCOLN'S PRIVATE 54
     QUARTERS

     Grant and Lincoln
     confer in grave, soft
     voices. Their words
     can't be made out. The
     aide stands at a          *
     respectful distance.      *

     Finally Lincoln
     straightens and shakes
     the general's hand.


55   INT. WHITE HOUSE       55
     CORRIDOR

     Grant and his aide pass
     back out the way they     *
     came in.
```

```
        GRANT - Rev. 1/7/04 92A.

56   EXT. VIRGINIA COUNTRY- 56
     SIDE - NIGHT

     Grant's special TRAIN
     CHUGS past in thick
     darkness, heading         *
     south.                    *
```

```
                             93.

57   EXT. DIRT ROAD - DAWN 57

     Grant rides astride a
     big gelding.  His
     aide trails him.
     They're riding fast,
     pushing their horses
     hard.


58   EXT. GRANT'S HEAD-        58
     QUARTERS - MORNING

     A hot sun is already
     shining.  A stir rises
     in the camp as Grant
     and his aide arrive.
     Grant dismounts and
     strides into his tent
     without a word to
     anyone.
```

Managing page numbers when a script is revised

As material is added and deleted over time, "A" pages are created, and other pages are deleted entirely, numbering the pages properly becomes essential to helping everyone keep their scripts in the correct order with the current version of each page.

The basic numbering scheme for pages is the same as it is for scenes:

> Between 5 and 6 comes 5A.
> Between 5A and 6 comes 5B.
> Between 5A and 5B comes A5B.

The principal is that page A5 precedes page 5 and page 5A follows page 5.

If an entire page of text is deleted, it's essential to account for the page number so that everyone knows what has become of the page. If half of page 5 and all of page 6 are deleted (and page 7 has no changes), we end up with a page numbered 5/6. Production personnel will then understand that they throw away old pages 5 and 6 and replace them with the new page 5/6.

If multiple pages are deleted, the entire range of deleted page numbers must still be accounted for. To that end, we can issue a page numbered 14-18. Production personnel will discard all of the pages in that range and replace them with the new page 14-18.

Title pages distributed with revisions

When revised pages are distributed, they always include a title page printed on the new color of paper and listing the date and color of the revision:

Rev. 03/09/04 (Pink)

UNDER THE TABLE

written by

Jose Patrick Sladkey

FINAL DRAFT

March 7, 2004

As the above example shows, the date and draft of the last full script remain listed in the lower right corner of the title page and the date and color of the revised pages appear in the upper right corner of the page.

The dates and colors of subsequent sets of revised pages get added to the list at the top right of the title page as they are issued, with the date in six-digit format to keep things lined up:

```
Rev. 03/09/04 (Blue)
Rev. 03/13/04 (Pink)
Rev. 03/20/04 (Yellow)
Rev. 03/20/04 PM (Green)
Rev. 03/21/04 (Gold)
```

This list of revised dates and colors remains on the title page until a new full draft of the script is issued, if ever.

Note in the example above that a second set of revisions issued in the course of a single day bears the notation "PM" to distinguish it from the first set.

For more on title pages, see the section on *Special Pages*.

SPECIAL PAGES

Special script pages include *title pages, cast pages, sets pages, first pages, last pages,* and pages containing *act breaks.*

Samples of many of these pages can be found in *Appendix C.*

■ Title pages

Every script needs a title page. The type of script will determine what information the title page should contain.

For a screenplay or teleplay written *on spec* (that is speculatively, not on assignment or under contract to a studio or producer), the title page should contain, at minimum, three pieces of information: 1) the title; 2) the name of the writer; and 3) contact information.

For a screenplay or teleplay written *under contract* to a studio or producer, the title page should contain 1) the title; 2) the name of the writer; 3) contact information, in this case the name of the studio or producer; and 4) the draft and date. It may also contain 5) a copyright notice.

1.   *Title*

The title is centered 4.0" below the top of the page, typed in all capital letters and underscored with one continuous underline. Quotation marks are not used.

GONE WITH THE WIND

For an episode of a television series, add the episode title, double-spaced beneath the series title, in upper and lower case letters, enclosed in quotation marks and underscored. The underline should not extend beneath the quotation marks.

LAW AND ORDER

"One for the Road"

2.   *Name(s) and credit of the writer(s)*

The writer's name and credit appear centered, beginning four lines below the title:

12 HOURS IN BERLIN

written by

Felix Alvin Butler Jr.

• *Name*

The writer's name is typed in upper and lower case letters. If multiple writers are working as a team, their names are joined by an ampersand (&):

Felicia Keyes & Matthew Scott Brown

• *Credit*

Screen credits in Hollywood are determined by the Writers' Guild of America following shooting. Prior to that official determination, WGA rules require that the title page list the names of all writers who have worked on the project. The name of the first writer comes first, beneath the credit "written by," "screenplay by," or "teleplay by." The names of subsequent writers follow, beneath the credit "revisions by." The name of the current writer comes last, beneath the credit "current revisions by":

12 HOURS IN BERLIN

written by

Felix Alvin Butler Jr.

revisions by

Maria Gustav
Charles Knowles-Hilldebrand
Robert Bush

current revisions by

Johann Potemkin

3. *Contact information*

For a spec script, you want the reader to know how to contact you if there's interest in your script. If you are not represented by an agent, manager or attorney, your address and/or phone number should appear in the lower left corner of the title page, beginning 1.2" from the left edge of the paper:

```
12902 Hollywood Place
Burbank, CA 91505
(818) 555-9807
```

For a script represented by an agent, manager, or attorney, leave the writer's information off. The representative's contact information will appear on the title page, script cover, or cover letter.

For a script written under contract, the studio or producer's contact information will appear:

```
MICHAEL GELD PRODUCTIONS
4000 Warner Boulevard
Burbank, CA 91505
```

4. *Draft and date*

In order to help distinguish one version of a script from another, a script in development, preproduction, or production ordinarily lists the script's draft and date in the lower right corner, beginning 5.5" in from the left edge of the paper. The draft is typed in all capital letters and underscored. The date is typed in upper and lower case letters, double-spaced beneath the draft:

FIRST DRAFT

March 3, 2003

A spec script has no real need to list a draft and date and can avoid appearing stale simply by leaving that information off the title page.

5. *Copyright notice*

Some studios and production companies list a copyright notice on title pages of their scripts. This notice appears directly beneath the draft and date:

REV. FINAL DRAFT

May 2, 2004
© 2004
MICHAEL GELD PRODS.
All Rights Reserved

Most spec scripts don't list a copyright notice or WGA registration number.

6. *When a script is based on other material or on a true story*

Information relating to source material for a script is listed beneath the writer's name, centered, in upper and lower case letters:

THE IMAGINARY WAR

screenplay by

Mari Zwick

based on the book by

Robert McMullen

Scripts based on, suggested by or inspired by true stories can indicate that fact in the same spot:

based on a true story

■ Cast pages

A cast page is usually included in an episodic television script at the preproduction stage. Some made-for-television movie scripts also incorporate cast pages. Feature film scripts and spec scripts do not.

A cast page follows the title page and lists the cast arranged either in order of appearance or according to some set order of regular cast, followed by the guest cast in order of appearance. The character names are typed in all capital letters at the left margin, beneath the title and the heading "CAST":

NINE LIVES

"Cats Away"

CAST

KITTY

JULIO MENDEZ

HILDE SCHMIDT

FELIX SIMPSON

LIEUTENANT MARTIN

For hour-long television and made-for-television movies, the list can wrap into a second column, if necessary.

Half-hour television scripts often include the names of the actors playing each role and a listing of any extras needed. The character name appears on the left side and the actor's name appears on the right. The names are connected by a dot leader:

<u>NINE LIVES</u>

"Cats Away"

<u>CAST</u>

KITTY.................................MARSHA WILLIAMS

JULIO MENDEZ...........................ALEX GONZALEZ

HILDE SCHMIDT......................ALISON PARMENTER

FELIX SIMPSON.................MICHAEL PAUL MILLIKAN

LIEUTENANT MARTIN.....................ANTHONY BOGNA

PARKING LOT EXTRAS
POLICE HEADQUARTERS EXTRAS

Cast pages are not numbered.

■ Sets pages

A sets page, like a cast page, is usually included in an episodic television script at the preproduction stage. Some made-for-television movie scripts also incorporate sets pages. Feature film scripts and spec scripts do not.

For hour-long television and made-for-television movies, interior sets are listed in a column on the left side of the page and exterior sets are listed in a column on the right:

<pre>
                        NINE LIVES

                      "Cats Away"

                         SETS

      INTERIORS: EXTERIORS:

      KENNEDY HIGH SCHOOL   PARK

      NEW YORK STOCK EXCHANGE   SCHOOL PLAYGROUND

      STORM SEWERS   NEW YORK STOCK EXCHANGE

                                DUMP
</pre>

Sets are grouped logically. For example, if scenes take place in several different locations inside an elementary school, they get listed like this:

<pre>
      HAMMOND ELEMENTARY SCHOOL
           Library
           Cafeteria
           Mrs. Timberlake's
             Classroom
</pre>

Sets pages are not numbered.

■ First pages

The first page of a script is unique in the following ways:

- Although it is counted as page 1, no page number is typed on the first page.

- The title is usually typed at the top of the first page, centered, in all capital letters and underscored. For episodic television, the episode title appears double-spaced beneath the series title, in upper and lower case letters, enclosed in quotation marks and underscored. The underline should not extend beneath the quotation marks.

- The first page virtually always begins with a FADE IN.

The first page of a script for a feature film or a made-for-television movie begins like this:

<u>THE LONG SLIDE</u>

FADE IN:

EXT. HIMALAYAS - HIGH ON WINDSWEPT PEAK

Snow and blinding sunshine.

The first page of an hour-long television episode begins like this:

<u>NINE LIVES</u>

"Cats Away"

<u>ACT ONE</u>

FADE IN:

EXT. PARK - DAY

KITTY sits high in the branches of a tree.

An example of the first page of a half-hour television script can be found in the section on *multi-camera film format*.

■ Last pages

The last page of a script concludes with the words "THE END" typed in all capital letters, underscored and centered. If space allows, leave five blank lines between the final transition (e.g. FADE OUT or CUT TO BLACK) and "THE END." If space doesn't allow the full five blank lines, leave at least one blank line.

> Kitty climbs back into the tree and watches as the dilapidated school bus disappears into the night.
>
> FADE OUT.

<u>THE END</u>

■ Act breaks

Scripts for episodic television shows and for many made-for-television movies contain act breaks, which represent the commercial breaks in the program. An hour-long television script usually consists of four acts. Half-hour scripts consist of either two or three acts. Two-hour movies typically consist of seven or eight acts. Some shows also include a teaser or prologue before the first act and/or an epilogue or tag after the last act.

A new act always begins at the top of a new page which includes a heading identifying the act in all capital letters, double-spaced beneath the page number, centered and underscored, followed by a transition double-spaced beneath it:

```
                                                        16.


                          ACT TWO


        FADE IN:


        INT. DETECTIVE BULLPEN - NIGHT


        Savage slams a case file down on his desk.  He picks up
        the phone and punches in a number.  He's not happy.
```

The last page of an act ends with a transition (usually FADE OUT) double-spaced below the final script text, followed by the words "END OF ACT ONE" (or TWO or THREE, etc.) typed in all capital letters, underscored and centered. If space allows, leave five blank lines between the final transition (e.g. FADE OUT or CUT TO BLACK) and "END OF ACT ONE." If space doesn't allow the full five blank lines, leave at least one blank line.

```
        Kitty races out the door in time to see McCloud
        wrestled aboard the bus.  She pulls her gun and
        sprints for the BUS but it ROARS away, leaving her
        in a cloud of dust

                                              FADE OUT.




                          END OF ACT FIVE
```

The last page of the entire script ends with no reference to the number of the current act. Instead, it ends with the words, "THE END." (See *Last pages* above.)

MULTI-CAMERA FORMAT

This is the format most often used today for half-hour comedies. Much of what is true of single-camera film format and discussed in detail earlier in this guide is also true of multi-camera film format:

- The margins for shot headings, direction, dialogue, and transitions are the same
- The same rules apply to font size and type, and paper size and type
- Shot headings are arranged according to the same rules
- The same rules apply to how dialogue and direction are broken between pages

The principal differences from single-camera film format are these:

- Shot headings and transitions are underscored
- Direction is typed in all capital letters
- Dialogue is double-spaced
- Sound cues are pulled out of direction and underscored
- Parenthetical character direction is embedded in dialogue

Each half-hour television series customizes the format somewhat, so it's helpful, if you wish to match a show's look exactly, to obtain a sample script from the series.

See *Appendix B* for sample script pages in multi-camera film format.

■ Standard multi-camera film format margins

Standard multi-camera film format margins are as follows:

1. **Paper** is 3-hole punched 8-1/2" x 11" white 20 lb. bond

2. **Shot headings:**
   Left margin is 1.7" (position 17)
   Right margin is 1.1" (position 73)
   Line length is 57 characters
   Shot headings are underscored

3.   **Direction:**
        Left margin is 1.7" (position 17)
        Right margin is 1.1" (position 73)
        Line length is 57 characters
        Direction is typed in all capital letters

4.   **Dialogue:**
        Left margin is 2.7" (position 27)
        Right margin is 2.4" (position 60)
        Line length is 34 characters
        Dialogue is typed in upper and lower case letters and
            double-spaced

5.   **Character name over dialogue:**
        Left margin is 4.1" (position 41)
           **Note that the character name over dialogue is not
           centered.** It begins at the same fixed point (4.1"
           from the left edge of the page) no matter how
           long it is

6.   **Parenthetical character direction** is embedded in dialogue in all capital letters

7.   **Scene transitions:**
        Left margin is 6.0" (position 60)
        Scene transitions are underscored

8.   **Sound cues:**
        Left margin is 1.4" (position 14)
        Right margin is 1.1" (position 73)
        Line length is 59 characters
        Sound cues are typed in all capital letters and underscored
           and begin with the abbreviation SFX:

9.   **Scene letters:**
        Go at 7.2" (position 72), on the line immediately
           following the page number
        Scene letters are capitalized and enclosed in parentheses

10.   **Page numbers:**
        Go at 7.2" (position 72), .5" below the top edge of
           the paper

11.   **Font:**
>   Courier or Courier New 12 point (or equivalent
>   fixed-pitch serif font)

12.   **Page length:**
>   60 lines (which allows for .5" margin at the top
>   and bottom of each page)
>
>   These 60 lines include one line at the top of each page for
>   the page number, followed by the scene letter, followed
>   by the text of the script

■ Shot Headings

Shot headings are arranged according to the principles detailed for single-camera film format. The only change for multi-camera format is that shot headings are underscored:

```
INT. "BETTER FRED THAN DEAD" DINER - DAY
```

Typically multi-camera format scripts use very few shot headings besides master scene headings. It is common for a scene to run in its entirety beneath a single heading.

A new scene always begins on a new page. However, when action moves continuously from one room to an adjacent room and cameras don't stop rolling, a new shot heading may be used without it being considered a new scene. In this case, the new shot doesn't indicate a new scene but only a new portion of a continuing scene. Drop four lines after the final text of the first portion and type the new shot heading, like this:

```
INT. DINER - KITCHEN - DAY
(Fred)

FRED POURS PANCAKE BATTER ON THE GRIDDLE.   TURNS ON
THE DISHWATER.  HE RUSHES OUT INTO:



INT. MAIN DINER

HE UNLOCKS THE FRONT DOOR.  RUSHES BACK INTO:
```

```
INT. KITCHEN

HE FLIPS THE PANCAKES.   THROWS DIRTY DISHES IN THE
SINK.
```

■ Direction

Direction is typed in all capital letters. This of course alleviates the need to decide what to capitalize and greatly simplifies the task of formatting multi-camera format scripts:

```
IT'S THE BREAKFAST RUSH.   FRED'S BEHIND THE COUNTER.
MARTHA'S TAKING AN ORDER FROM DEBBIE, EARLY 20S,
ATHLETIC, LEAN.
```

Underscoring character entrances and exits

Character entrances and exits are underscored in direction. Underscore the name of the character and the word or words describing the entrance or exit:

```
THE DOOR OPENS.   BOB ENTERS.

CURT COMES THROUGH THE FRONT DOOR AND SLIPS ON A
BANANA PEEL.

BEICHMAN GRABS A BUCKET AND EXITS AT A RUN.
```

Underscoring camera direction

Camera direction is underscored in direction. Underscore the word camera as well as any words related to the camera's movement and associated prepositions:

```
SWEETPEA SITS ALONE ON A CHAIR, READING THE LETTER.
HER BODY IS RACKED WITH SILENT SOBS.   CAMERA PULLS
BACK TO REVEAL THAT THE ENTIRE ACTING CLASS
SURROUNDS HER, WIPING AWAY TEARS AT HER BRAVURA
PERFORMANCE.
```

■ Dialogue

Character names over dialogue follow the same rules as those for single-camera film format. The dialogue itself is typed in upper and lower-case letters and double-spaced:

                        FRED

        That's it! First Johnny called and

        said he had the flu. Now Ronnie

        calls with a cold. The job is a

        real headache.

                        MARTHA

        I've gotta tell you. All this

        moaning and groaning is making me

        sick!

Using (CONT'D) when dialogue continues after an interruption

Whenever the same character continues speaking after an interruption for direction or a sound cue, the abbreviation (CONT'D) is placed beside the character's name over dialogue, typed in all capital letters, inside parentheses:

                        DEBBIE

        Ronnie, come over here.

    RONNIE APPROACHES, FILLED WITH TREPIDATION.

                        DEBBIE (CONT'D)

        Come closer. I'm not gonna hurt

        you.

■ Parenthetical character direction

All the rules from single-camera film format apply here, with one important exception. In multi-camera format, parenthetical character direction is embedded in the dialogue, not pulled out on a separate line at a separate tab:

```
                    FRED

        Eyes this way, people.  (WAITS)

        So that's about it.  (TURNS TO

        O.S. AUDIENCE) How'd we do?
```

■ Transitions

Scene transitions follow the same rules in multi-camera format that they do in single-camera film format. The only difference here is that they get underscored:

<u>CUT TO</u>:

<u>WIPE TO</u>:

<u>DISSOLVE TO</u>:

<u>FADE OUT</u>.

<u>RIPPLE DISSOLVE TO</u>:

■ Sound cues

All *sound cues* (sounds that must be made by someone besides an actor on camera) are pulled out of direction, underscored and typed at a margin that begins three spaces to the left of the margin for ordinary direction, preceded by the abbreviation "SFX":

```
    CURT HITS THE FLOOR.  MOANS LIKE A COW.

 SFX: THE PHONE RINGS.

    NO ON ANSWERS IT.  CURT LOOKS UP FROM WHERE HE LIES
    ON THE FLOOR.
```

■ Character listings

Characters who appear in a scene are listed beneath the shot heading for that scene. They are typed in the order of appearance, in upper and lower case letters, inside parentheses, with extras listed after speaking characters:

```
INT. "BETTER FRED THAN DEAD" DINER - DAY
(Fred, Martha, Bob, Debbie, Curt, Diner Extras)

IT'S THE BREAKFAST RUSH.   FRED'S BEHIND THE COUNTER.
MARTHA'S TAKING AN ORDER FROM DEBBIE.
```

■ Scene numbers or letters

Scenes in a multi-camera script are either lettered or numbered. Most often they are lettered. The scene letter appears capitalized, inside parentheses, on each page of the scene.

First page of a scene

Practices vary from series to series, but the following is a common and time-honored scheme. On the first page of a scene, the scene letter is centered, 12 lines below the top of the page. The text of the scene begins 12 lines below that:

21.

(D)

INT. FRED'S APARTMENT - NIGHT
(Fred, Martha)

FRED ENTERS TO FIND MARTHA TRYING TO WRESTLE THE
REFRIGERATOR OUT AN OPEN WINDOW.

Subsequent pages

All subsequent pages that are part of the scene show the scene letter directly
below the page number. The text of the script begins on the line immediately
below the scene letter:

45.
(G)

CURT PLACES THE CHAIRS ON TOP OF THE TABLES.

■ First pages of acts

Like hour-long television and many made-for-television movies, half-hour television scripts are divided into acts. Some also include a teaser or prologue and a tag or epilogue.

Page one

The first page of a multi-camera script includes the series and episode titles plus the heading ACT ONE, TEASER or PROLOGUE, as appropriate, typed in all capital letters, underscored and centered:

BETTER FRED THAN DEAD

"A Simple Sample"

ACT ONE

(A)

FADE IN:

INT. "BETTER FRED THAN DEAD DINER - DAY
(Fred, Martha, Debbie, Bob, Curt, Diner Extras)

IT'S THE BREAKFAST RUSH. FRED'S BEHIND THE COUNTER.
MARTHA'S TAKING AN ORDER FROM DEBBIE.

The scene letter appears on line 12 and the text of the script begins on line 24. As with single-camera film format, the page number is not typed on page 1.

First pages of subsequent acts

The first page of each subsequent act begins with the act heading (e.g. ACT TWO) typed in capital letters, centered and underscored on line 3, followed by the scene letter on line 12 and the text of the script beginning on line 24:

```
                                                  30.


                     ACT THREE




                       (G)








FADE IN:

INT. CURT'S TAXI - NIGHT
(Curt, Customer Extra)

CURT DRIVES.  HE'S WHISTLING A TUNE.  AT FIRST IT'S
HARD TO MAKE OUT WHAT IT IS.
```

Last page of each act

The last page of an act ends with a transition (usually FADE OUT) double-spaced below the final script text, followed by the words "END OF ACT ONE" (or TWO or THREE, etc.) typed in all capital letters, underscored and centered. If space allows, leave five blank lines between the final transition (e.g. FADE OUT or CUT TO BLACK) and "END OF ACT ONE." If space doesn't allow the full five blank lines, leave at least one blank line.

```
FRED CLOSES THE DOOR TO THE DINER AND SHUTS OFF THE
LIGHTS.

                                             FADE OUT.




              END OF ACT ONE
```

The last page of the entire script ends with no reference to the number of the current act. Instead, it ends with the words, "THE END."

■ Breaking pages

The following rules govern the breaking of pages in multi-camera film format scripts.

No CONTINUEDs

When a scene continues from one page to the next, no (CONTINUED) is placed at the bottom of one page and no CONTINUED: appears at the top of the next. The scene simply continues.

Breaking dialogue

When a speech is broken at the bottom of a page, always break at the end of a sentence and add (MORE) at the bottom of the first page, double-spaced beneath the dialogue, and (CONT'D) at the top of the following page beside the character name:

> CURT
>
> This is the last time I come in
>
> here expecting to be served
>
> something that's actually, how
>
> do you say, edible.
>
> (MORE)

12.
(B)

> CURT (CONT'D)
>
> Can I just have a bottle of water
>
> and some crackers?

Even when direction interrupts the speech, (MORE) and (CONT'D) are still required:

> FRED
>
> Comin' atcha.
>
> HE CLIMBS ONTO THE DINER COUNTER.
>
> (MORE)

7.
(A)

> FRED (CONT'D)
>
> Yo. Yo yo. Your attention right
>
> here, if you please.

Note that (MORE) is typed beneath the interrupting line of direction, as the last word on the page.

Breaking direction

When breaking direction from one page to the next, always break at the end of a sentence:

```
CURT CLIMBS TO HIS FEET.  FRED CLAPS HIS HANDS FOR
ATTENTION.
```

```
                                                  24.
                                                  (E)
EVERYONE IN THE DINER STANDS, FACES CURT AND APPLAUDS.
```

Breaking near a sound cue

When breaking a page near a sound cue, arrange the break so that the sound cue is not the first item at the top of a page. If a sound cue won't fit at the bottom of a page, carry it to the top of the next page along with the dialogue or direction that immediately precedes it:

```
CURT COMES THROUGH THE FRONT DOOR AND SLIPS ON THE
BANANA PEEL.  HE TAKES OUT AN ENTIRE ROW OF TABLES
ON HIS WAY DOWN.  IT'S A SIGHT TO BEHOLD.
```

```
                                                  3.
                                                  (A)


                    DEBBIE

          I stand corrected.

SFX: THE PHONE RINGS.

NO ONE ANSWERS IT.  CURT LOOKS UP FROM WHERE HE LIES
ON THE FLOOR.
```

Breaking near a shot heading

A shot heading can't appear as the last item at the bottom of a page. At least one full sentence of direction must accompany the shot heading or it should be moved to the top of the next page.

Breaking before a scene transition

Never break a page immediately before a transition. If a transition won't fit at the bottom of a page, carry it to the top of the next page along with the dialogue or direction that immediately precedes it:

```
                                                        4.
                                                       (A)
        EVERYONE IN THE DINER STANDS, FACES THE AUDIENCE AND
        BOWS.


                                        DISSOLVE TO:
```

UNDERWOODS & APPLES: TOOLS OF THE SCREENWRITING TRADE

Photographers need cameras. Painters need brushes. And screenwriters need computers. We used to need typewriters, but that was a long time ago. Now we need computers. *Need* them. And why is that exactly? What do computers do for us that typewriters never could?

As we begin a discussion about computer hardware and software, it's useful to review the job this technology should be doing for us as it relates to putting our scripts on the page.

■ Back in the day...

In the beginning there were Underwoods. Big, noisy monstrosities that had the remarkable ability to put words on paper in whatever order and configuration the writer wished, including standard screenplay format. No batteries ever ran low. There was no toner to buy, no drum unit, no ink cartridge, no software upgrade. The keyboard and printer were built into the device and the thing was virtually incapable of jamming or breaking down. Once in a while a ribbon needed to be replaced. Other than that, the Underwood just spit out script pages.

Unfortunately, if you wanted to add a line, delete a word, or flip-flop the order of two paragraphs, you had to retype the whole page. Often you had to retype the whole dang script. Either that or cut and paste with literal scissors and cellophane tape. And you had to find your own typos by actually reading the page you'd written. And correcting the typos you found was no picnic. And if your finished screenplay fell off the copy boy's bicycle on the way to the mimeo department and blew away, well, it was simply gone. The only backup copy was locked somewhere in your imperfect memory.

■ Flash forward to the wired and wireless future

Today, of course, everything has changed. The Underwood is a relic and the wireless home network is here. Let's review what the new machines have brought to our big Hollywood party:

- Computers let us make changes to an existing script page with ease, which means we no longer have to weigh the physical difficulty of making a script change. We just do it.

- Computers loaded with script-typing software provide automatic margin changes as we move effortlessly from dialogue to direction to shot headings and back again.

- Computers allow us to spell-check our work and can give us access to an electronic dictionary and thesaurus and even screenwriting advice.

- Computers provide crisp, flawless original printouts of script pages, free from white-out smudges and erasure holes.

- Computers can print as many of those flawless originals as we like.

- Computers provide numerous ways for us to back up our work and protect it from rain, flood, fire – and a few viruses the Underwood never seemed to catch.

- Computers even allow us to transmit our scripts electronically and virtually instantaneously anywhere in the world, opening up unimagined doors of possibility for collaboration.

There's no question we're immensely better off with computers. The challenge is making sure we reap the maximum benefit from the technology without surrendering control of the final product to a piece of computer equipment or programming. We mustn't trade our ability to create script pages that are correctly and professionally formatted for pages that are simply easy to produce. Which brings us to the next part of our discussion.

■ What computers can't do

A computer can't write your movie for you. Obviously. No more than the paintbrush can create a masterpiece without the artist. But here's what we sometimes miss. A computer can't *format* your script for you, either.

Surprised?

Look back at the list above. Yes, computers armed with good software will apply standard margins to a shot heading or a scene transition. But the software can't tell you where to put the shot heading, what information to include, what to leave out. It can't help you with sound or camera capping in direction. It can't tell you where to paragraph or what belongs in parenthetical character direction or whether you ought to underscore or capitalize or italicize words in dialogue for emphasis. It won't tell you that your establishing shot isn't really an establishing shot, or that you need to yank Huck out of Huck's POV. All of that has to come from you. From your knowledge of standard Hollywood script format. Computer software, by itself, will never be enough. Don't ask it to do a job it was never designed to do.

■ Choosing the right software

So which program should you use? It depends on who you are and what you want the software to do.

The first rule of choosing computer software to use in writing scripts is simply this: **Choose the program that best helps you put your script on the page.** That's its job. To help you, the writer, put the words where you want them, not where the software wants them. If a program is preventing you from laying out your script the way you see fit, if it's dictating to you and inhibiting your control over your own work, then it's the wrong program.

Second, **choose the program that provides the features you need.** Are you going to be writing spec scripts only? Then you don't necessarily need software that meets the rigorous demands of production. Are you working with a writing partner? Choose a program that's compatible with your partner's. Are you typing scripts for a television series in production? You need software that allows you to control the numbering of scenes and pages, the placement of revision marks and the content of the revision slug.

You have several programs to choose from.

Do-it-yourself software solutions

Many writers work within a robust word processing software like Microsoft Word or WordPerfect, using a personalized set of macros and styles to apply margins to their scripts. Warner Bros. has for many years used a complex set of macros in conjunction with WordPerfect for typing scripts. This approach allows a computer-savvy writer maximum control over the various elements of a script but provides less automation than commercial script software.

Commercial script software

Many other writers swear by one of several commercial script-typing programs on the market ranging in price from about $50 to $250. Some are complete, stand-alone programs:

- Final Draft

- Movie Magic Screenwriter

- Scriptware

- Page 2 Stage

Others work within Microsoft Word:

- HollyWord

- Script Wright

- ScriptWerx

- Script Wizard

Each of these programs automates various parts of the script-typing process. The features of various programs are constantly evolving, but usually include many of the following:

- Preset margins for screenplays (what I call in this manual "single-camera film format"), sitcoms ("multi-camera film format"), and stage plays.

- Import/export of files to and from various common file formats, including Rich Text Format, Adobe Acrobat, and HTML.

- Automatic typing of repeated character names and master shot headings (e.g. you type CAPT and the software completes CAPTAIN VON TRAPP)

- Spell check

- Thesaurus

- Index card systems that allow for the simplified reshuffling of scenes

- Online writing advice about such things as plot, structure, and character

- Automatic revision marks

- A and B scene and page numbers

- Colored pages for revisions

Of the commercial script-typing programs currently on the market, Final Draft is the best-selling. That carries certain benefits, among them file compatibility with large numbers of other writers and producers. But you should choose the program with the features that are important to the way you are going to work. And don't settle for software that doesn't allow you to put the words where you know they belong.

■ Don't let the autopilot fly you into the ground

Many writers get lulled into believing that their scripts are professionally formatted simply because they're typed using a best-selling script program. They're wrong. As helpful as these programs are, the writer is still the writer. If the software wants to add "(continuing)" every time a character's dialogue is interrupted by direction, don't let it. You know better. If the software's autotype feature wants to repeat precisely the same master scene heading every time you return to a location, don't let it. You're the writer. You know better. You decide what goes in the shot heading. Don't let the computer make creative decisions for you. That isn't its job. It's yours. You're the writer. You know better.

■ Mac vs. PC

As fraught with emotion as this question sometimes becomes, this is an easy one. Writers use both Macintosh and IBM-PC based computers. Both work. Choose a computer that runs the software you want to use and is compatible with anyone with whom you expect to collaborate.

■ Printers

If there are still any dot-matrix printers out there, put them out of their misery. Laser-quality printing is standard in Hollywood. That means a true laser printer (Brother sells one for less than $200) or a good inkjet printer capable of at least

600 dpi (available from Epson and Canon, among others, for well under $100). Never send out a page that doesn't look perfect.

■ Backup

One of the great benefits of typing scripts on a computer is that you can easily save copies of every draft and keep multiple backups in multiple locations to prevent the catastrophic loss of your work due to fire or some other disaster. Don't neglect to back up your work. You're investing countless hours of creativity in a script that, if not properly safeguarded, can disappear at the speed of light.

While you're writing

Make sure the autosave feature is enabled and is frequently backing up your work as you go, at least once every ten minutes. The worst that can happen, in the event of a power failure or computer crash, is that you'll lose ten minutes' worth of work.

When you quit for the day

Before you walk away from your computer, back up your work to a removable medium, either a floppy disk, a CD, a tape drive, or even a paper printout — something that will survive if your hard drive doesn't. This ensures that the worst that can happen, even if the hard drive dies in the middle of the day, is that you'll lose only one day's work.

At least once a week

Store a backup copy of your script at a remote location. That can mean a paper copy, floppy, or CD kept in the car or office, or a copy of the file stored in free online storage such as that provided by Yahoo. That way, even if your computer and box of diskettes melt in a fire or get crushed by stampeding bison, your script will endure.

File-naming protocol

If you're working as hard as you should be, you'll produce numerous drafts of each project you write. The best way to keep all those files straight is to use a set file-naming protocol. Here's mine.

First I give the project a short name. Let's say my movie is called PEARL HARBOR SAVED MY LIFE. For purposes of backup, I'll call the project PEARL. The very first version of the project will get saved as PEARL01, with whatever file extension is appropriate, such as .doc or .fdr. The next version will be PEARL02. Then comes PEARL03. That's all there is to it. It's simple, it's easy, the file names stay short, and I never have to guess which version came when.

When to change the file version number

How often should you give the file a new name by increasing the version number, changing PEARL05 to PEARL06? As often as necessary to maintain a record of what you've written. Let's say you start PEARL05 as a page-one rewrite. On the first day you write pages 1 through 4. The next day you keep going and write pages 5 through 8. No need to rename the file. You're only building on the existing draft. Just keep saving the growing file under the name PEARL05. But then one day after you reach page 60, you decide to go back and revise the first half of your movie. Now you want to increase the version number so that you keep a record of those first 60 pages. Rename the file PEARL06 before you make your changes. If you ever want to go back and look at something from PEARL05, you'll have it.

A Final Word

Screenplays and teleplays are more than technical documents. They are a form of literature in their own right, separate from the films and television programs that may be made from them. And just as the layout of a poem on the page is an integral part of the poetry, so format is an integral part of the art of the script.

Use the guidelines in this manual as a launching point for your creativity. Properly understood, they should never hold you back. Instead, use the principles contained in this book as tools *to free you* to express clearly and powerfully your artistic vision, to capture on the script page the best and deepest and truest things you know.

Write with all your heart. Advance the art of the screenplay.

APPENDIX A

■ Single-camera film format

Sample Script Pages

PERFECT PITCH

FADE IN:

EXT. VAN NUYS APARTMENT - MORNING

A 12-year-old tagger, not unlike a pit bull, leaves his
mark on a fire hydrant outside this dreary stucco
complex.

It's a picture-perfect day in the Valley. Not a cloud in
the beige sky.

An ALARM CLOCK GOES OFF.

INT. STUDIO APARTMENT

A feminine arm shoots out of the covers and gropes a
bedside table for the ALARM. Knocks a pair of glasses
onto the floor. Keeps searching. Tips an empty coffee
mug onto its side. Finally finds the clock and hits
snooze. The ALARM GOES SILENT.

The arm drops back onto the bed.

The ALARM CLOCK TICKS.

VENETIAN BLINDS

RATTLE almost imperceptibly.

OVERTURNED COFFEE MUG

rocks gently back and forth.

WIDE ON APARTMENT

Silence for the longest time. Then all hell breaks
loose.

The ROOM SHAKES VIOLENTLY. The bed hops like a spastic
rabbit. Pictures drop off the walls.

The COFFEE MUG falls and SHATTERS.

ASPIRING SCREENWRITER

explodes from beneath the covers, eyes wide with terror as her APARTMENT QUAKES around her. GRETCHEN PFLUM.

Beside her bed a computer monitor sways violently, tips and topples.

Gretchen dives. Gets tangled in the sheets. Hits the floor just as the MONITOR SMASHES over the top of the printer.

And then it ALL STOPS. Just like that. Gretchen looks around the apartment. It's an unbelievable mess. So's she. Early 20s, she's rumpled and badly shaken. But so darn cute you don't care.

Seven seconds of silence. And then the PIPES over her head BURST. WATER DRENCHES the apartment.

EXT. GRETCHEN'S APARTMENT - MORNING

The door is flung open. Gretchen staggers outside. Rumpled, shaken and now soaked. But still cute. CAR ALARMS are BLARING. DOGS are BARKING. Neighbors are spilling from their apartments. Gretchen looks around, spots an elderly woman in a muumuu.

                    GRETCHEN
          Stella, what just happened? What
          was that?!

STELLA toddles toward Gretchen, utterly unruffled.

                    STELLA
          Oh, I'd say about a six point one
          or six point two. Have a muffin, dear.
                    (hands Gretchen one
                     and glances at her
                     watch)
          Didn't you have a meeting this
          morning?

Gretchen blanches.

                         GRETCHEN
              Oh no.

INT. GRETCHEN'S APARTMENT

She appears in the doorway. WATER continues to RAIN DOWN.

                         GRETCHEN
              Oh no.

She plunges into the room.

Steps over fallen items to her computer. Sees the
shattered monitor atop the printer.

                         GRETCHEN
              OH NO.
                    (a cry from the
                     depths)
              MY PITCH!!!!!!!!!!

She starts to dig. Heaves the monitor to the floor. Her
PHONE RINGS. She looks for it. Can't find it. It KEEPS
RINGING. In frustration she kicks the monitor shell.
Unearthing the phone. She answers.

                         GRETCHEN
              Hello?

                         GRETCHEN'S MAMA (V.O.)
              Baby?

INTERCUT WITH:

EXT. KANSAS FARM - ENDLESS WHEAT FIELD - DAY

GRETCHEN'S MAMA in the air-conditioned, glassed-in
cockpit of a massive, modern combine, mowing down wheat.
She's got a cell phone to her ear. A RADIO PLAYS LOW in
the b.g.

                         GRETCHEN
              Mama?

GRETCHEN'S MAMA
Listen, baby, I can't talk long
but I want you to Fed Ex me some
more of that good mango salsa.

Gretchen picks gingerly through the broken glass that
litters her computer equipment. She pulls a stack of
soggy pages from the printer.

GRETCHEN'S MAMA
Your father and I drizzled it over
our grilled salmon last night
and --

GRETCHEN
(starting to cry)
Mama, I just had an earthquake.

GRETCHEN'S MAMA
An earthquake? Are you sure, baby?

GRETCHEN
(crying harder)
Of course I'm sure --

GRETCHEN'S MAMA
Because I've got on C.N.N. and
they're not saying a thing about
an earthquake.

Gretchen looks at the destruction all around her.
Doesn't know what to say.

GRETCHEN
Mama, I've got to go. I have a
very important meeting and I
overslept and then the earthquake
woke me up --

GRETCHEN'S MAMA
Well there you go! Blessing in
disguise.
(then)
Gotta go, baby. Don't forget the
salsa. Kisses.

She clicks off. Leaving Gretchen remembering why she fled Kansas in the first place.

                                        CUT TO:

EXT. APARTMENT BUILDING - PARKING LOT - GRETCHEN'S CAR - DAY

A WHIMPERING sound as Gretchen rushes up, dressed, her hair still wet. She hears the sound and looks around. Sees nothing. Unlocks her door. The WHIMPERING again. She looks beneath her car.

HER POV UNDER CAR

A dirty, frightened CHIHUAHUA cowers, CRYING.

                    GRETCHEN (O.S.)
          Hey there, Taco Bell, what's
          wrong?

BACK TO SCENE

Gretchen extends her arms. The dog races from under her car and leaps into them. She laughs.

                    GRETCHEN
          Earthquake scare you, little guy?
                    (beat)
          Listen, I've got to run. Where do
          you belong?

The little dog licks her face.

EXT. STUDIO GATE - DAY

Gretchen pulls up to the guard shack in her '83 Civic. A GUARD steps up to the car.

                    GUARD
          Going to see?

                    GRETCHEN
                (intimidated)
        Ian von Blitzenkrantz.

                    GUARD
        The producer?
                (looks over her sad
                 little car)
        Here to dust his Oscars?

Something rises up inside Gretchen. She is, after all, a
screenwriter.

                    GRETCHEN
        No, I'm not here to dust his Oscars.
        I'm here to win him another one.

The Guard is duly impressed by her moxy.

                    GUARD
        Name?

                    GRETCHEN
        Gretchen Pflum. P-F-L-U-M.

The Guard checks his list.

                    GUARD
        Don't see it.
                (looks inside car)
        And you can't bring in the dog.

The little chihuahua sits on the passenger seat. Eating
Gretchen's pitch.

                    GRETCHEN
        No, no, no!!!

She pulls the half-eaten pages from the dog's mouth.
They're beyond salvage.

                    GRETCHEN
        Oh noooooooooo!!!

INT. PRODUCER'S OFFICES - RECEPTION AREA - DAY

A hard-driving young executive WANNA-BE jabbers into a
telephone headset while he surfs the Web. Everything he
says he says fast.

                        WANNA-BE
              Von Blitzenkrantz Entertainment...
              He'sinameetingcanwereturn?

He looks up as Gretchen enters.

                        WANNA-BE
                   (to phone)
              Holdplease.
                   (to Gretchen)
              Helpyou?

                        GRETCHEN
              Gretchen Pflum. I have a meeting
              with Mr. von Blitzenkrantz. I
              may be a little, um... late.

                        WANNA-BE
              HaveaseatI'lllethimknowyou'rehere.
              Wantanythingtodrink?
              Coffeesodawater?

Gretchen takes a beat to decode his spiel.

                        GRETCHEN
              Oh. Well. Um. Water.

She smiles.

                        WANNA-BE
              Bottled or tap?

                        GRETCHEN
              Oh. Um. Bottled.

                        WANNA-BE
              Perrier or Evian?

                        GRETCHEN
              ... Perrier.

> WANNA-BE
> Room temperature or refrigerated?

Gretchen just stares.

                                        DISSOLVE TO:

INT. RECEPTION AREA - LATER

Time has passed. Lots of time. The bottle of Perrier is
empty. Gretchen's trying to piece together what's left
of her tattered pitch. The Wanna-Be is still on the phone.

> WANNA-BE
> NoIhaven'treadthescriptI'vereadthe
> coverage. Greatcoverage. Huge
> coverage. BestcoverageI'veever
> read. PluginOrlandoorMattorWill
> andyou'vegotahit.

                                        DISSOLVE TO:

INT. RECEPTION AREA - LATER

The Wanna-Be is gone. Gretchen still waits. Finally, a
voice like a foghorn bellows from O.S.

> VOICE (O.S.)
> Jason?!... Jason?!... Jason?!...
> Jason?!

A puffy-faced guy in his 50s pads out in his bare feet.
IAN VON BLITZENKRANTZ. He sees there's no one behind the
desk. Spots Gretchen.

> VON BLITZENKRANTZ
> Who are you?

> GRETCHEN
> Gretchen Pflum. I'm supposed to
> pitch to Mr. von Blitzenkrantz.

He stares at her an uncomfortably long moment. At long,
long last:

> VON BLITZENKRANTZ
> Okey-dokey.

INT. VON BLITZENKRANTZ'S OFFICE - DAY

Movie posters from his Oscar-winning films cover the
walls. Statuettes litter the desk. Gretchen sits on the
couch, dry-mouthed and tongue-tied, leafing through the
pages of her prepared pitch. Von Blitzenkrantz waits.

                    VON BLITZENKRANTZ
          So, sweetheart. Now's when you
          tell me a story.

Gretchen looks up like a deer caught in the headlights.
Clears her throat. Sets the pages aside. And begins.

                    GRETCHEN
          A studio apartment in Van Nuys.
          An alarm clock is ringing.
          There's a girl --

                    VON BLITZENKRANTZ
          How old?

                    GRETCHEN
          Early twenties.

                    VON BLITZENKRANTZ
          Good. We'll get that chick from
          "Alias."

                    GRETCHEN
          The girl's in bed. She's
          overslept.

                    VON BLITZENKRANTZ
          Who's she with?

                    GRETCHEN
          Who's she with? Um... she's
          alone.

                    VON BLITZENKRANTZ
          She's alone?
                    (guffaws)
          How interesting is that?!
                    (then)
          No, seriously.

                    GRETCHEN
        Well... okay... she's not
        completely alone. There's a dog.

                    VON BLITZENKRANTZ
        What kind of dog?

                    GRETCHEN

        Chihuahua.

                    VON BLITZENKRANTZ
        Chihuahuas are hot right now. I
        like the way you think.

                    GRETCHEN
        Then this massive earthquake hits.
        <u>BANG</u>!!!

She slams her hand down on the coffee table. Von
Blitzenkrantz nearly jumps out of his skin. He cocks his
head and studies Gretchen. At long last throws his hands
straight up in the air and exclaims:

                    VON BLITZENKRANTZ
        <u>I love this stuff</u>!!!
                (stands)
        I gotta pee.
                (heads for the door)
        But you keep going. You're doing
        great.

He disappears. Gretchen looks around the empty office.
Shrugs. And keeps going.

                    GRETCHEN
        So the bed starts jumping around
        like a spastic rabbit, the girl is
        like insane with fear --

Gretchen gets up and crosses to the enormous desk.
Admires the Oscars there.

                    GRETCHEN
        But she doesn't care, she's got
        the first pitch meeting of her
        life and nothing is going to stop
        her.

She spots a little dust on one of the statuettes. Buffs it with her sleeve.

                    GRETCHEN
          But then she sees her computer
          monitor about to crash onto her
          only copy of her perfect,
          wonderful pitch. She dives! <u>And
          snatches that bad boy out of the
          air</u>!!!

Gretchen smiles like the sunrise. 'Cause she's in Hollywood now.

                                        FADE OUT.

                         <u>THE END</u>

APPENDIX B

■ **Multi-camera film format**

Sample Script Pages

BETTER FRED THAN DEAD

"A Simple Sample"

ACT ONE

(A)

FADE IN:

INT. "BETTER FRED THAN DEAD" DINER - DAY
(Fred, Martha, Debbie, Bob, Curt, Diner Extras)

IT'S THE BREAKFAST RUSH. FRED'S BEHIND THE COUNTER.
MARTHA'S TAKING AN ORDER FROM DEBBIE, EARLY 20S,
ATHLETIC, LEAN.

                    DEBBIE
          Ham and cheese omelet, side of

          bacon, coffee.

                    MARTHA
          (KNOWING) Atkins diet.

                    DEBBIE
          Yes, ma'am.

                    MARTHA
          (CALLS TO FRED) Ham and cheese

          omelet, bacon.

                    FRED
          Comin' atcha.

HE CLIMBS ONTO THE DINER COUNTER.

                    (MORE)

> FRED (CONT'D)

Yo. Yo yo. Your attention right
here, if you please. As you may
know, we're all appearing in a
half-hour multi-camera television
production.

> MARTHA

(LOOKING PAST CAMERA) That would
explain the live audience in the
bleachers, Fred.

> FRED

Yes it does.

THE FRONT DOOR OPENS. BOB ENTERS.

> FRED (CONT'D)

What it doesn't explain is the
deplorable lack of humorous
dialogue, pratfalls and the like.

BOB SLIPS ON A BANANA PEEL AND HITS THE DECK IN A
MASTERFULLY EXECUTED BIT OF PHYSICAL COMEDY.

> FRED (CONT'D)

I stand corrected.

> MARTHA

So anyway --

                    FRED

    So anyway, what we have here is a

    little piece of situation comedy.

    A simple little sample, as it

    were. But lacking a certain

    je ne sais quoi.

                    MARTHA

    There, you've said it. What we

    have here --

                    FRED

    Is a situation.

                    MARTHA

    Without the comedy.

CURT COMES THROUGH THE FRONT DOOR AND SLIPS ON THE BANANA
PEEL. HE TAKES OUT AN ENTIRE ROW OF TABLES ON HIS WAY
DOWN. IT'S A SIGHT TO BEHOLD.

SFX: THE O.S. AUDIENCE LAUGHS.

                    DEBBIE

    I stand corrected.

SFX: THE PHONE RINGS.

    NO ONE ANSWERS IT. CURT LOOKS UP FROM WHERE HE LIES ON
    THE FLOOR.

                    CURT

    Anyone going to help me up?

DEBBIE

Nope.

FRED

Not a chance.

MARTHA

Don't look at me. The longer

you're on the floor, the funnier

it gets.

SFX: THE AUDIENCE HOWLS.

CURT CLIMBS TO HIS FEET. FRED CLAPS HIS HANDS FOR
ATTENTION.

FRED

Eyes this way, people. (WAITS)

So that's about it. (TURNS TO

O.S. AUDIENCE) How'd we do?

SFX: HUGE APPLAUSE.

EVERYONE IN THE DINER STANDS, FACES THE AUDIENCE AND BOWS.

DISSOLVE TO:

■ **Title, Cast, and Sets Pages**

Sample Script Pages

This is a simple title page for a spec feature script with only one writer and no source material. This is all the information that's required.

PERFECT PITCH

written by

Gretchen Pflum

12902 Hollywood Place
Burbank, CA 91505
(818) 555-9807

This is a typical title page for an episode of a television series with two writers working as a team. The title pages for both hour and half-hour series are identical.

BETTER FRED THAN DEAD

"A Simple Sample"

written by

John Gretel & Isaac Mott

JOSHUA McMANUS PRODUCTIONS
Bungalow 15
10202 W. Washington Boulevard
Culver City, CA 90232

REV. FIRST DRAFT

August 2, 2004

Rev. 07/13/04 (Blue)
Rev. 07/15/04 (Pink)
Rev. 07/16/04 (Yellow)
Rev. 07/21/04 (Green)

This is a title page for a feature film in production and includes the names of all participating writers, the draft and date, and a listing of dates and colors for all sets of revised pages included in the current draft.

12 HOURS IN BERLIN

written by

Felix Alvin Butler Jr.

revisions by

Maria Gustav
Charles Knowles-Hilldebrand
Robert Bush

current revisions by

Johan Potemkin

FINAL DRAFT

July 12, 2004
© 2004
MICHAEL GELD PRODS.
All Rights Reserved

MICHAEL GELD PRODUCTIONS
4000 Warner Boulevard
Burbank, CA 91505

<u>NINE LIVES</u>

<u>"Cats Away"</u>

<u>CAST</u>

KITTY

JULIO MENDEZ

HILDE SCHMIDT

FELIX SIMPSON

LIEUTENANT MARTIN

MAX

REBECCA BEAKER

GUARD #1

GUARD #2

DR. SRINIVASAN

LYLE

SAM

TODD

MRS. BRACKMAN

ROTO-ROOTER GUY

This is a cast list for an episode of a one-hour television series. The speaking characters are listed in order of appearance. It is also common to list the series regulars first, followed by the rest of the cast in order of appearance. Extras are not listed. A cast page is not numbered.

NINE LIVES

"Cats Away"

CAST

KITTY.................................MARSHA WILLIAMS

JULIO MENDEZ.............................ALEX GONZALEZ

HILDE SCHMIDT........................ALISON PARMENTER

FELIX SIMPSON...................MICHAEL PAUL MILLIKAN

LIEUTENANT MARTIN.......................ANTHONY BOGNA

GUEST CAST

MAX...TIM FISH

REBECCA BEAKER...........................SYLVIA SIMMS

GUARD #1................................N. KELLY LYON

GUARD #2.................................JAMES BEISE

PARKING LOT EXTRAS
POLICE HEADQUARTERS EXTRAS

A typical cast list for an episode of a half-hour television series looks like this. Character names are listed on the left and actors' names are listed on the right. The regular cast often appears in a set order, with guest cast listed in order of appearance. Extras are listed in order of appearance below the guest cast. A cast page is not numbered.

NINE LIVES

"Cats Away"

SETS

INTERIORS:

KENNEDY HIGH SCHOOL
  Main Office
  Science Lab
  Library
  Girls' Bathroom

NEW YORK STOCK EXCHANGE

STORM SEWERS

POLICE HEADQUARTERS
  Holding Cell
  Detectives' Bullpen

McDONALD'S RESTAURANT

STAPLES CENTER
  Escalator
  Luxury Suite
  Basketball Court
  Visitors' Locker Room

FUNERAL HOME

EXTERIORS:

PARK

SCHOOL PLAYGROUND

NEW YORK STOCK EXCHANGE

DUMP
  Front Gate

SOUTH L.A. STREETS

POLICE HEADQUARTERS

McDONALD'S RESTAURANT

STAPLES CENTER

CEMETERY

VENICE BEACH

This is a sets list for a one-hour television drama. Primary locations are listed in order of appearance, with secondary locations grouped beneath each primary location. A sets page is not numbered.

NINE LIVES

"Cats Away"

SETS

Teaser, Scene A - Int. Detectives' Bullpen - Day

Act One, Scene B - Int. Kitty's Apartment - Kitchen - Night

Act One, Scene C - Int. Kitty's Apartment - Bedroom - Night

Act One, Scene D - Int. Detectives' Bullpen - Morning

Act Two, Scene E - Int. Empire State Building - Elevator - Later That Day

Act Two, Scene F - Int. Detectives' Bullpen - Same Time

Act Two, Scene G - Int. Empire State Building - Lobby - 30 Minutes Later

Tag, Scene H   - Int. Kitty's Apartment - Night

This is an example of a sets list for a half-hour television series. These pages, in particular, can take many forms, but virtually always each scene number or letter is listed in order along with its location, even when that means repeating locations. Sets pages are not numbered.

INDEX

ABOUT THE AUTHOR

Christopher Riley is a professional screenwriter working in Hollywood with his wife and writing partner, Kathleen Riley. Together they wrote the 1999 theatrical feature *After the Truth*, a multiple-award-winning German language courtroom thriller. The film sparked international controversy when it was released in Germany and earned its star Goetz George a best actor nomination for the prestigious European Film Award for his portrayal of Nazi doctor Josef Mengele. Since then, the husband-wife team has written scripts ranging from legal and political thrillers to action-romances for Touchstone Pictures, Paramount Pictures, Mandalay Television Pictures, and Sean Connery's Fountainbridge Films.

The author worked from 1983 to 1998 in the acclaimed Warner Bros. script processing department where he learned from veteran script proofreaders and typists with decades of Hollywood experience. He rose to manage the historic studio's script operation, supplying scripts to countless projects in development and production at Warner Bros. and virtually every other studio in Hollywood. He wrote the software used by the studio to type thousands of television and feature film scripts and he served as the final arbiter of standard script format for the studio.

In addition to writing, the Rileys train aspiring screenwriters for work in Hollywood and have taught in Los Angeles, Chicago, Washington, D.C., New York, and Paris. Together with their four children, they live in Los Angeles.

The author can be reached by e-mail at criley@scriptHollywood.com.

Introducing `scriptHollywood.com`

the online home of *The Hollywood Standard*

➤ find answers to script formatting questions submitted by readers

➤ submit your own script formatting questions to Christopher Riley, author of *The Hollywood Standard*

➤ get expert help developing your screenplay from consultants who are professional screenwriters – not readers – working *right now* in Hollywood

➤ obtain professional script typing and formatting services from veteran script typists who will conform your script to *The Hollywood Standard*

➤ contact screenwriters Christopher and Kathleen Riley about workshops and seminars on topics that include *The Heart of the Character-Driven Story*, *Theme and Meaning* and *My Big Fat Hollywood Idea*

⇒ find links to the most useful screenwriting sites on the web

Former screenwriting students say:

> "The Rileys constantly made me dig deeper into the characters and go for the emotional truth. Thanks to their input, I now have a fellowship at Disney and a script that gets managers and agents to call me."
>
> *Amy Snow*
> *Winner, 2004 Disney Fellowship*

> "My screenwriting took gigantic leaps forward under the Rileys' guidance. Their teaching style is so full of warmth and humor you don't realize at first how much you're being pushed toward greater depth and truth in your writing. I got from the Rileys not only clear, highly practical tools that improved my work immediately, but also rich insights into the broader truths of storytelling which will continue to inform my writing in the future."
>
> *Haynes Brooke*
> *playwright and screenwriter*

www.scriptHollywood.com

PSYCHOLOGY FOR SCREENWRITERS
BUILDING CONFLICT IN YOUR SCRIPT

WILLIAM INDICK, PH.D.

To make their stories come alive, screenwriters must understand human behavior. With this book, they can employ Sigmund Freud, Carl Jung, Alfred Adler, Erik Erikson, and Joseph Campbell as their writing partners. *Psychology for Screenwriters* helps scribes craft psychologically resonant characters and conflict. You'll learn to create convincing motivation, believable identity development, and archetypes that produce screen moments that ring true.

William Indick clearly describes theories of personality and psychoanalysis, with simple guidelines, thought-provoking exercises, vivid film images, and hundreds of examples from classic movies that resonate with the power of credible storytelling.

"You cannot find a clearer or more concise guide on the psychology of cinema than this book. A brilliant and insightful companion for the screenwriter and film aficionado alike. This lucid and lyric guide provides a 'let's go' tour of the most powerful psycho-literary theories of our age as they apply to hundreds of great films."
> — Marcus C. Tye, Ph.D.
> Clinical Psychologist, Associate Professor of Psychology

"Not just a book for screenwriting. It's a must book for anyone interested in the filmmaking industry. Indick provides a complete guide to understanding the psychology behind the plot, character development, and art of storytelling."
> — Robert C. DeLay
> Writer, Cedar Grove Agency Entertainment

"Here's a textbook for all those interested in creating emotionally charged stories and motivated characters. Using a mix of psychology, philosophy, and popular film, Dr. Indick helps writers delve into their stories through the minds of their characters — and their audiences."
> — Theresa Schwegel
> www.absolutewrite.com

WILLIAM INDICK is a screenwriter, author, and assistant professor of psychology at Dowling College.

$26.95 | 281 PAGES | ORDER # 122RLS | ISBN: 0-941188-87-6

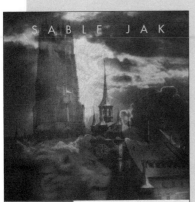

WRITING THE FANTASY FILM
HEROES AND JOURNEYS
IN ALTERNATE REALITIES

SABLE JAK

Think Fantasy films are limited to B movies and cheesy Sunday matinees? Think again. The Fantasy film genre has contributed major blockbuster motion pictures to the movie-going public for generations, from the *Star Wars* films to the *Harry Potter* hits and *The Lord of the Rings* trilogy.

Encompassing movies such as *It's a Wonderful Life* and the Science Fiction/Fantasy hybrid *The Matrix*, Fantasy is not bound by a specific formula. It spans all genres, times, and localities, and has contributed to the folklore and literature of every culture around the world. This book guides the screenwriter through the Fantasy script process — without having to sprinkle the fairy dust.

"*Finally, someone has tackled the genre that has fascinated and mystified screenwriters for decades. Long-time Scr(i)pt contributor Sable Jak deconstructs the fantasy genre and examines it on every level, from characters and quests to magic and mystery. No writer preparing to embark upon the epic journey of writing a Fantasy script should start without this literary talisman.*"
— *Shelly Mellott, Editor*
Scr(i)pt Magazine

"*An awesome resource that takes the mystery out of writing one of today's most popular film genres. Filled with tips, techniques, examples, and exercises that will fire up the imagination, Sable Jak's book leaves no stone — or Stonehenge — unturned.*"
— *Marie Jones, Book Reviewer*
www.absolutewrite.com

The astonishing success of *The Lord of the Rings* trilogy and other Fantasy films shows that the Fantasy film genre is going to be a dominant force in movie theatres for years to come. This book will help you create and write a saleable screenplay in this highly competitive category.

SABLE JAK is a Seattle-based writer for *Scr(i)pt Magazine* and *www.absolutewrite.com*. She is a life-long devotee of the Fantasy genre.

$26.95 | 220 PAGES | ORDER # 123RLS | ISBN: 0-941188-96-5

COULD IT BE A MOVIE?
HOW TO GET YOUR IDEAS OUT OF YOUR HEAD AND UP ON THE SCREEN

CHRISTINA HAMLETT

Includes a 50% discount certificate on professional script coverage – a $450 value!

Movies. No matter their theme, budget or cast, they all start out in pretty much the same way: with dreamers — just like you — sitting in darkened theaters around the world and imagining what it would be like to see their names scrolling up the credits after the words, "Screenplay Written By..."

Is there a movie inside of you that's been yearning to get out but you don't know where to begin? Before you stock your shelves with books on how to write a film, take this roadmap to determine if film is the best destination for your creative ideas.

This detailed book will teach you:
- How to identify whether your plot packs enough punch to be a hit movie.
- How to acquire and adapt pre-existing material for a feature length screenplay.
- How to find today's hot markets for the kind of films you want to write.
- How to predict what tomorrow's audiences will want to see.
- How to find and land an agent.

"The single most important thing about a screenplay is the basic concept. And the single most important thing an aspiring screenwriter can do is read this book before he or she starts writing."
    — Pamela Wallace
        Academy Award Winner (Witness) and Author

"Hamlett has culled together essential screenwriting information and integrated it with her wise industry counsel. Both will get you pointed in the right direction for being a successful screenwriter, and keep you there once you've arrived."
    — John E. Johnson
        Executive Director, American Screenwriters Association

CHRISTINA HAMLETT is an award-winning author and script coverage consultant whose credits include numerous books, plays, musicals, optioned features, and screenwriting columns.

$26.95 | 280 PAGES | ORDER # 21RLS | ISBN: 0-941188-94-9

THE WRITER'S JOURNEY
2ND EDITION
MYTHIC STRUCTURE FOR WRITERS

CHRISTOPHER VOGLER

BEST SELLER
OVER 116,500 UNITS SOLD!

See why this book has become an international bestseller and a true classic. *The Writer's Journey* explores the powerful relationship between mythology and storytelling in a clear, concise style that's made it required reading for movie executives, screenwriters, playwrights, scholars, and fans of pop culture all over the world.

Both fiction and nonfiction writers will discover a set of useful myth-inspired storytelling paradigms (i.e., "The Hero's Journey") and step-by-step guidelines to plot and character development. Based on the work of Joseph Campbell, *The Writer's Journey* is a must for all writers interested in further developing their craft.

The updated and revised second edition provides new insights and observations from Vogler's ongoing work on mythology's influence on stories, movies, and man himself.

"This book is like having the smartest person in the story meeting come home with you and whisper what to do in your ear as you write a screenplay. Insight for insight, step for step, Chris Vogler takes us through the process of connecting theme to story and making a script come alive."

> — Lynda Obst, Producer
> Sleepless in Seattle, How to Lose a Guy in 10 Days
> Author, Hello, He Lied

"This is a book about the stories we write, and perhaps more importantly, the stories we live. It is the most influential work I have yet encountered on the art, nature, and the very purpose of storytelling."

> — Bruce Joel Rubin, Screenwriter
> Stuart Little 2, Deep Impact, Ghost, Jacob's Ladder

CHRISTOPHER VOGLER, a top Hollywood story consultant and development executive, has worked on such high-grossing feature films as *The Lion King*, *The Thin Red Line*, *Fight Club*, and *Beauty and the Beast.* He conducts writing workshops around the globe.

$24.95 | 325 PAGES | ORDER # 98RLS | ISBN: 0-941188-70-1

MYTH AND THE MOVIES
DISCOVERING THE MYTHIC STRUCTURE OF 50 UNFORGETTABLE FILMS

STUART VOYTILLA
FOREWORD BY CHRISTOPHER VOGLER
AUTHOR OF *THE WRITER'S JOURNEY*

BEST SELLER
OVER 15,000 UNITS SOLD!

An illuminating companion piece to *The Writer's Journey*, *Myth and the Movies* applies the mythic structure Vogler developed to 50 well-loved U.S. and foreign films. This comprehensive book offers a greater understanding of why some films continue to touch and connect with audiences generation after generation.

Movies discussed include *The Godfather, Some Like It Hot, Citizen Kane, Halloween, Jaws, Annie Hall, Chinatown, The Fugitive, Sleepless in Seattle, The Graduate, Dances with Wolves, Beauty and the Beast, Platoon*, and *Die Hard*.

"Stuart Voytilla's Myth and the Movies *is a remarkable achievement: an ambitious, thought-provoking, and cogent analysis of the mythic underpinnings of fifty great movies. It should prove a valuable resource for film teachers, students, critics, and especially screenwriters themselves, whose challenge, as Voytilla so clearly understands, is to constantly reinvent a mythology for our times."*

— *Ted Tally, Academy Award Screenwriter*, Silence of the Lambs

"Myth and the Movies *is a must for every writer who wants to tell better stories. Voytilla guides his readers to a richer and deeper understanding not only of mythic structure, but also of the movies we love."*

— *Christopher Wehner, Web editor*
The Screenwriters Utopia *and* Creative Screenwriting

"I've script consulted for ten years and I've studied every genre thoroughly. I thought I knew all their nuances – until I read Voytilla's book. This ones goes on my Recommended Reading List. A fascinating analysis of the Hero's Myth for all genres."
— *Lou Grantt*, Hollywood Scriptwriter Magazine

STUART VOYTILLA is a screenwriter, literary consultant, teacher, and author of *Writing the Comedy Film.*

$26.95 | **300 PAGES** | **ORDER # 39RLS** | **ISBN: 0-941188-66-3**

FILM & VIDEO BOOKS

Cinematic Storytelling: *The 100 Most Powerful Film Conventions Every Filmmaker Must Know* / Jennifer Van Sijll / $24.95

Complete DVD Book, The: *Designing, Producing, and Marketing Your Independent Film on DVD* / Chris Gore and Paul J. Salamoff / $26.95

Complete Independent Movie Marketing Handbook, The: *Promote, Distribute & Sell Your Film or Video* / Mark Steven Bosko / $39.95

Costume Design 101: *The Business and Art of Creating Costumes for Film and Television* / Richard La Motte / $19.95

Could It Be a Movie?: *How to Get Your Ideas Out of Your Head and Up on the Screen* / Christina Hamlett / $26.95

Creating Characters: *Let Them Whisper Their Secrets* Marisa D'Vari / $26.95

Crime Writer's Reference Guide, The: *1001 Tips for Writing the Perfect Crime* Martin Roth / $20.95

Cut by Cut: *Editing Your Film or Video* Gael Chandler / $35.95

Digital Filmmaking 101: *An Essential Guide to Producing Low-Budget Movies* Dale Newton and John Gaspard / $24.95

Digital Moviemaking, 2nd Edition: *All the Skills, Techniques, and Moxie You'll Need to Turn Your Passion into a Career* / Scott Billups / $26.95

Directing Actors: *Creating Memorable Performances for Film and Television* Judith Weston / $26.95

Directing Feature Films: *The Creative Collaboration Between Directors, Writers, and Actors* / Mark Travis / $26.95

Eye is Quicker, The: *Film Editing; Making a Good Film Better* Richard D. Pepperman / $27.95

Fast, Cheap & Under Control: *Lessons Learned from the Greatest Low-Budget Movies of All Time* / John Gaspard / $26.95

Film & Video Budgets, 4th Updated Edition Deke Simon and Michael Wiese / $26.95

Film Directing: Cinematic Motion, 2nd Edition Steven D. Katz / $27.95

Film Directing: Shot by Shot, *Visualizing from Concept to Screen* Steven D. Katz / $27.95

Film Director's Intuition, The: *Script Analysis and Rehearsal Techniques* Judith Weston / $26.95

Film Production Management 101: *The Ultimate Guide for Film and Television Production Management and Coordination* / Deborah S. Patz / $39.95

Filmmaking for Teens: *Pulling Off Your Shorts* Troy Lanier and Clay Nichols / $18.95

First Time Director: *How to Make Your Breakthrough Movie* Gil Bettman / $27.95

From Word to Image: *Storyboarding and the Filmmaking Process* Marcie Begleiter / $26.95

Hitting Your Mark, 2nd Edition: *Making a Life – and a Living – as a Film Director* Steve Carlson / $22.95

Hollywood Standard, The: *The Complete and Authoritative Guide to Script Format and Style* / Christopher Riley / $18.95

I Could've Written a Better Movie Than That!: *How to Make Six Figures as a Script Consultant even if You're not a Screenwriter* / Derek Rydall / $26.95

Independent Film Distribution: *How to Make a Successful End Run Around the Big Guys* / Phil Hall / $24.95

Independent Film and Videomakers Guide – 2nd Edition, The: *Expanded and Updated* / Michael Wiese / $29.95

Inner Drives: *How to Write and Create Characters Using the Eight Classic Centers of Motivation* / Pamela Jaye Smith / $26.95

I'll Be in My Trailer!: *The Creative Wars Between Directors & Actors* John Badham and Craig Modderno / $26.95

Moral Premise, The: *Harnessing Virtue & Vice for Box Office Success* Stanley D. Williams, Ph.D. / $24.95

Myth and the Movies: *Discovering the Mythic Structure of 50 Unforgettable Films* / Stuart Voytilla / $26.95

On the Edge of a Dream: *Magic and Madness in Bali* Michael Wiese / $16.95

Perfect Pitch, The: *How to Sell Yourself and Your Movie Idea to Hollywood* Ken Rotcop / $16.95

Power of Film, The Howard Suber / $27.95

Psychology for Screenwriters: *Building Conflict in your Script* William Indick, Ph.D. / $26.95

Save the Cat!: *The Last Book on Screenwriting You'll Ever Need* Blake Snyder / $19.95

Screenwriting 101: *The Essential Craft of Feature Film Writing* Neill D. Hicks / $16.95

Screenwriting for Teens: *The 100 Principles of Screenwriting Every Budding Writer Must Know* / Christina Hamlett / $18.95

Script-Selling Game, The: *A Hollywood Insider's Look at Getting Your Script Sold and Produced* / Kathie Fong Yoneda / $16.95

Selling Your Story in 60 Seconds: *The Guaranteed Way to get Your Screenplay or Novel Read* / Michael Hauge / $12.95

Setting Up Your Scenes: *The Inner Workings of Great Films* Richard D. Pepperman / $24.95

Setting Up Your Shots: *Great Camera Moves Every Filmmaker Should Know* Jeremy Vineyard / $19.95

Shaking the Money Tree, 2nd Edition: *The Art of Getting Grants and Donations for Film and Video Projects* / Morrie Warshawski / $26.95

Sound Design: *The Expressive Power of Music, Voice, and Sound Effects in Cinema* / David Sonnenschein / $19.95

Stealing Fire From the Gods, 2nd Edition: *The Complete Guide to Story for Writers & Filmmakers* / James Bonnet / $26.95

Storyboarding 101: *A Crash Course in Professional Storyboarding* James Fraioli / $19.95

Ultimate Filmmaker's Guide to Short Films, The: *Making It Big in Shorts* Kim Adelman / $16.95

What Are You Laughing At?: *How to Write Funny Screenplays, Stories, and More* / Brad Schreiber / $19.95

Working Director, The: *How to Arrive, Thrive & Survive in the Director's Chair* Charles Wilkinson / $22.95

Writer's Journey, – 2nd Edition, The: *Mythic Structure for Writers* Christopher Vogler / $24.95

Writer's Partner, The: *1001 Breakthrough Ideas to Stimulate Your Imagination* Martin Roth / $24.95

Writing the Action Adventure: *The Moment of Truth* Neill D. Hicks / $14.95

Writing the Comedy Film: *Make 'Em Laugh* Stuart Voytilla and Scott Petri / $14.95

Writing the Killer Treatment: *Selling Your Story Without a Script* Michael Halperin / $14.95

Writing the Second Act: *Building Conflict and Tension in Your Film Script* Michael Halperin / $19.95

Writing the Thriller Film: *The Terror Within* Neill D. Hicks / $14.95

Writing the TV Drama Series: *How to Succeed as a Professional Writer in TV* Pamela Douglas / $24.95

DVD & VIDEOS

Field of Fish: *VHS Video* Directed by Steve Tanner and Michael Wiese, Written by Annamaria Murphy / $9.95

Hardware Wars: *DVD* / Written and Directed by Ernie Fosselius / $14.95

Sacred Sites of the Dalai Lamas – DVD, The: *A Pilgrimage to Oracle Lake* A Documentary by Michael Wiese / $22.95